# The Essential Guide to Buying and Selling Luxury Real Estate

## *Insights from America's Top Luxury Agents*

Dana Rice
Moira E. Holley
Liz Harris
Nancy Tallman
Tom Tezak
Bruce Jones
Mark Cain
Joshua Baris
Elena Price
Alex Gandel

Copyright © 2018 NMG Publishing

All rights reserved. No portion of this book may be reproduced mechanically, electronically or by any other means without the expressed written permission of the publisher, except as provided by the United States of America copyright law.

Published by NMG Publishing, Charlotte, North Carolina.

The authors and publisher have strived to be as accurate and complete as possible in the creation of this book.

This book is not intended for use as a source of legal, accounting, or financial advice. The information in this book is intended to provide basic information on the topics covered and is not intended to be comprehensive by any means. All readers are advised to seek legal and financial advice from competent professionals, including real estate agents or brokers, when making decisions related to any real estate purchase, sale, or investment, or any other topics covered in this book. The authors and publisher are not responsible or liable for any damages or negative consequences to any person reading or following the information in this book.

The opinions expressed in this book are not those of the publisher. Each co-author contributed to this book in their own personal capacity and the views they have expressed in this book are their own individual views, not the views of the publisher, nor of the other co-authors.

A REALTOR® is a real estate professional who is a member of the National Association of REALTORS® and subscribes to the association's Code of Ethics. The word REALTOR® is not used to describe a person working in the real estate field who is not a member of the National Association of REALTORS®.

While all attempts have been made to verify information provided in this publication, the authors and publisher assume no responsibility for errors, omissions, or contrary interpretation of the subject matter herein. Any perceived slights of specific persons or organizations are unintentional.

Any trademarks mentioned in this book are listed for reference purposes only and are the property of the respective trademark owners.

# Table of Contents

Introduction . . . . . . . . . . . . . . . . . 1

Dana Rice:
Buying and Selling Luxury Homes
in Metro Washington, D.C. . . . . . . . . . . . . . . . 3

Moira E. Holley:
Buying and Selling Luxury Homes in Seattle . . . . . . . . 21

Liz Harris:
Buying and Selling Luxury Homes
in Highlands and Cashiers, NC . . . . . . . . . . . . . . 43

Nancy Tallman:
Buying and Selling Luxury Homes in Park City, Utah . . . . . 57

Tom Tezak:
Buying and Selling Luxury Homes on Maui . . . . . . . . 75

Bruce Jones:
Buying and Selling Luxury Homes in Nashville . . . . . . . 95

Mark Cain:
Buying and Selling Luxury Homes in the Dallas Area . . . . .115

Joshua Baris:
Buying and Selling Luxury Homes in Northern New Jersey. . .133

Elena Price:
Buying and Selling Luxury Homes
in the Suburban Boston Area . . . . . . . . . . . . . .155

Alex Gandel:
Buying and Selling Luxury Homes
in Ventura County and the San Fernando Valley. . . . . . .173

# Introduction

According to the National Association of REALTORS® there are over 1.3 million real estate agent or broker members in the United States. A very small percentage of agents and brokers focus significantly on the luxury real estate market, which is generally viewed as the top 10% of homes in the local market. Values range into the multiple million-dollar price range—a significant financial asset for owners or buyers. The publisher has selected 10 of the top luxury agents and brokers from around the United States to contribute to this book. Each of the contributors has a high volume of completed transactions, is highly rated by their clients, and is an advocate for their clients' success. The contributors are spread out geographically from Hawaii to the East coast and represent a mix of metro and resort/vacation locations. Each contributor has provided their insights for luxury home buyers and sellers in their area. We hope that this book will become a useful reference for consumers interested in buying or selling luxury homes around the United States.

NMG Publishing

# Introduction

According to the National Association of REALTORS® there are over 1.3 million real estate agent or broker members in the United States. A very small percentage of agents and brokers focus significantly on the luxury real estate market, which is generally viewed as the top 10% of homes in the local market. Values range into the multiple million-dollar price range—a significant financial asset for owners or buyers. The publisher has selected 10 of the top luxury agents and brokers from around the United States to contribute to this book. Each of the contributors has a high volume of completed transactions, is highly rated by their clients, and is an advocate for their clients' success. The contributors are spread out geographically from Hawaii to the East coast and represent a mix of metro and resort/vacation locations. Each contributor has provided their insights for luxury home buyers and sellers in their area. We hope that this book will become a useful reference for consumers interested in buying or selling luxury homes around the United States.

NMG Publishing

# Buying and Selling Luxury Homes in Metro Washington, D.C.

## Dana Rice

### Introduction

Armed with a degree in journalism and years of sales success at Fortune 500 companies, Dana Rice brings a storyteller's touch and reporter's insight to the marketing of homes.

A real estate investor at first, Dana bought, renovated, and sold a number of properties for her own account. With the decision to make real estate a full-time profession, Dana formed the Dana Rice Group, affiliated with Compass in Washington, D.C. where she is Senior Vice President, and has been named one of *Washingtonian's* Best Agents and Top Producers since the inception of her business.

Although Dana and her group represent buyers and sellers in the wider Metro Washington, D.C. area, her key focus is in Northwest Washington, D.C. and surrounding areas of

Bethesda and Chevy Chase, Maryland. She is a long-time resident of Bethesda, is involved in the local community, and has an intimate knowledge of real estate in her area of focus.

In this chapter, Dana Rice provides insight to buyers and sellers of luxury homes in the Washington, D.C. area.

## Selling Your Metro Washington Area Luxury Home

The real estate industry has become marvelously transparent. Photos, virtual tours, floorplans, 3-D rendering, and websites that estimate home values, create an abundance of data points that often contradict each other. Like most fields today, information is now an essential commodity, and the true value of this commodity is in the interpretation. In local real estate, this is even more relevant.

The first step is for a home seller, even in the earliest of stages, to engage in conversation with a real estate agent. Most luxury homeowners are highly productive. They likely have a great track record in their own profession and are used to managing things on their own; however, an experienced agent can provide useful insight on market conditions that make a difference when selling a home. Even if the owner is considering selling in a few years, it can be helpful to start getting educated on the market and important trends that will help them in the long term.

More importantly, it may keep the seller from the pain of investing money into a renovation or project that hurts the sale in the future. It is not uncommon for a homeowner to find out their selection of tile or paint color could be a repellant to an offer.

Pricing a property strategically is the most important factor in getting the highest price when selling. Period. Every market has its own cadence, and in the Metro Washington area, accurate pricing is critical in attracting offers. In other markets, it may be common to float a high, unrealistic price and expect rounds of negotiations once an offer is submitted. In D.C., that just isn't the case—buyers just view unrealistic pricing as a waste of time. They will not take the seller seriously and not bother to write an offer. This can be detrimental to the seller as reducing the price later and extending days on market puts doubt in the buyers' minds: *Is something wrong with the property? Why isn't anyone else making offers?*

Market pricing is also dynamic. It moves quickly. And it can change overnight. The classic supply and demand factors are in play on the larger stage of local real estate with the number of contracts being written, the number of homes on the market, and how well each is presented. When working with a seller, we review market data weekly, sometimes daily, as we prepare a property for the market. We have one chance to ensure we have the best pricing strategy, so we study the data in real time.

As for location, it is a real estate cliché for good reason. Location is the primary factor in determining real estate value. While school district tends to be a significant driver of interest, "walkability" and convenience to core shopping and transportation districts are even greater influencers. Amenities such as coffee shops, bike paths, smaller shopping venues for convenience are all part of daily living, and local restaurants factor in buyer decisions more than ever. Every home is unique and with the majority of homes in the area being older, there's more of an art of placing an appropriate price on a home than in newer, more homogenous developments.

Let's look at an actual case study of a home in Bethesda, Maryland. A rather unique property, this 138+ year old farmhouse is located in a close-in suburb of the city. It stands out as one of the few remaining original 1800s farmhouses in the area on an oversized lot. With its soft, yellow color and wide, wrap around porches, it is well known and liked by most people driving by. But, how to price? The analysis was challenge due to the lack of comparable properties. We started with simple data to strip away the emotional part of the analysis: number of bedrooms and bathrooms, square footage, and lot size. Then we looked for trends in farmhouses within a broader radius. Once we determined the valuation of each of these, and as there were so few comparables, we looked within a certain radius from core transportation and shopping hubs. This particular property is about one-half mile from a Metro station. Once we measured in concentric rings around Metro stations, it was clear to see a trend for premium pricing of any type of property within a certain distance to the Metro. Once the impersonal data was gathered, we then layered in the emotional components. How to present the heart, soul, and feelings of this home? What is a buyer looking for who would pay more than a million dollars for an old farmhouse? Every home has a "story" and it's more than just numbers. It's a feeling in the buyers' minds that creates excitement and desire. We developed a narrative. or story, about what was unique about this home, highlighted these factors in our descriptions, in materials provided to agents, in our social media platforms with live broadcasts, and created materials from actual historic documents that fleshed out generations of history. At one point, the great-great-grandson of the original owner stopped in to share even more about the home. With all this in play, there was significant interest and we received five offers. The home was sold to the highest bidder with the strongest terms possible, and both seller and buyer came away thrilled in the process.

When a home is on the market, we ask sellers to think of their property as a Wal-Mart or Target. Not because we want them to discount anything, but because the home is now a physical, retail establishment designed to welcome buyers (or "shoppers") at every turn, just like any retail store. This is especially critical in the luxury market. Luxury buyers tend to be the most discerning, most demanding, and most unforgiving in the presentation of a property. Every detail matters in this junction between buyer and seller, especially overall condition of the house. Buyers want reassurance that the property is well maintained, and they cannot easily examine internal systems like plumbing, heating and air conditioning, and electrical, so they make judgments based on what can be seen. Prior to entering the market, sellers should keep paint touched-up, leaks tightened and repaired, clutter removed, lights on, and bathrooms cleaned. Fair or not, buyers judge on how much effort was put into these simple things nearly as much as the important maintenance of major systems.

One simple buyer courtesy that reinforces a seller's commitment to home maintenance is for a seller to create a binder or list of service providers like lawn and yard service, HVAC, pool maintenance, and others and to present to the buyers. Buyers may want to check with some of your service companies to get a better feel for the level of maintenance and may be interested in continuing service with the people who are most familiar with your property.

Regardless of price point, my team provides "white glove" service to all of our clients. When a seller wants and needs to squeeze the most value out of a home, prepping it for sale can often be a full-time job. Just like any industry, when clients employ experts and engage with those who consistently perform in the arena, they will have better results.

Most sellers are overwhelmed by the process, but it does not have to be so daunting with a fully implemented strategy. Our team simply starts by arriving with our designer and walking room by room with the seller.

We provide design and staging services complimentary to all of our clients because only through the eyes of the strategist and the artist will the whole package come together. Once through the home, we provide a checklist with bulleted points of tasks in each room. Then the seller and I sit down to determine who should do the work. The seller, always in control of the process, will use these blueprints or plans as the framework under which we're going to get the house ready for sale. Sometimes my team will do the work like managing handymen, landscapers, and estate sales people. The sellers will employ a company, or do it themselves. But in the end, everybody has a straightforward plan of attack to ensure the property will garner the most money in the sale.

What is eye-opening to sellers is that we actually need to sell the home twice over… once online to internet shoppers, and once to the buyers when they come to the house. We employ a professional architectural photographer who understands composition, lighting, and how to tell a story with pictures. This is not a time or place to use a mobile phone camera! With the advent of more sophisticated photo technology, online tours, and 3-D models, we are competing beyond the neighborhood or the metropolitan area. And in the buyers' minds, the effort sellers put forth in presenting the property once again reinforces the opinion of the homeowner overall.

In addition to the images and home presentation, actual buyer access to the property is a critical component in the transaction. This may seem intuitive, but with multiple parties wanting to tour the property, we try to protect our sellers from too much inconvenience. It's not easy running a household in addition to the logistics of buyer tours. With the right strategy, we work to consolidate the time needed for the tours, and condense the time in the market with proper pricing and proper presentation. Working closely with the sellers, their family members and household employees like nannies or housekeepers, we encourage easy access through online scheduling of appointments, electronic lockbox access, and detailed instructions allowing for all parties' convenience.

Home sales are currently brisk and swift in the D.C. metropolitan area, but that does not mean that everything sells magically. The best course of action is to cast the widest net possible. Sellers must enter the market with a "bang," as it is the most exciting time for the buyers. We launch to the market with dedication to perfection from the moment the buyer sees our property – photo spreads, open houses, direct mail, social media broadcasts, online campaigns with proven targeting, descriptions that engage and invite, with some good old-fashioned networking with agents. Sellers have one moment to be great, and all the effort leads to this moment. This is the intersection of novelty and excitement.

On the other side of this marketing coin, is the "private exclusive" offering or "whisper listing." The lack of inventory means that sellers who are more discreet or private have the option to offer their property to active buyer groups before entering into the multiple listing service. It may seem counter-intuitive, but utilizing the same marketing toolkit of photo tours, floorplans, marketing brochures, we can test a certain list price before it hits the MLS. Because technology has finally caught up to the general marketplace, real estate offers can be shared far and wide through a multitude of planforms without inhibiting exposure to the most qualified buyer groups.

In the end, the offer is just the first step in the complicated process of contract to close. But once we have presented the home in its very best light, we find the transactions smoothly close with all parties in agreement.

## What Sellers Are Saying

*"Seriously the gold standard of Realtors. Dana and her team exude the perfect mix of professionalism, cutting edge savvy, resourcefulness, and comfort. I struggled with two other realtors for an entire year before hiring Dana. Dana made me feel like I was her ONLY client and put forth unbelievable effort. I trusted her implicitly and knew it would be the one decision I made that year that I would never regret. Her team of professionals, who specialize in the details, turned my house into a jaw dropper. (If I were on Love it or List it...I would have had a very hard time!) For me, it was her action-oriented style and her realness that I will always remember. I know that when I'm ready to do this house thing again, I know where to find her."*
    - User69671243

"We chose Dana Rice from Compass Real Estate Chevy Chase office to list and sell our property in Bethesda, MD, during May 2016. Dana's responsiveness during the entire transaction stands out as the key attribute she brings to the home sales process. Along with Dana's extensive knowledge and experience of the overall market, she provides a powerful combination of personality and professionalism. Our home listed on the market just 4 days, and we received 5 competing bids that closed almost 10% above list price.

"Dana made an immediate, positive impact when she identified the original architect of our house and highlighted the hallmark features incorporated into many of his homes in the neighborhood. She used these architectural features to create photos and advertising copy that attracted savvy buyers, eventually landing a contract because the buyers were architecture aficionados. Dana lives in the same neighborhood so she understood precisely how to market our property for maximum visibility and profit. We were initially disappointed with Dana's suggested list price, but she provided a compelling explanation of her market analysis. And the ultimate sales results were truly outstanding and exceeded our expectations.

"Dana invested every effort to answer our questions quickly and thoroughly. Her insight and suggestions always yielded better understanding of the listing and sales process. Her team of associates and sales resources at Compass was knowledgeable and informative. The entire transaction beginning to end proceeded smoothly and without complication. As an added benefit, Dana's positive energy and humor kept the stressful experience of downsizing and selling both upbeat and stress-free.

"We highly recommend Dana Rice for her responsiveness, her expertise, and her unrelenting positive spirit. Dana gets results!"
- hpollitt

"Dana is an exceptional realtor! She really knows her stuff, her business, and the local market. She also has a great team working with her, which is a huge asset and makes the process much easier. We couldn't be more pleased with her services; you really won't be disappointed!"
- Neil Fanton

## Buying Your Metro Washington Area Luxury Home

We sometimes say to our buyers, "If you see it in the MLS, it's probably too late." While exaggerated to make a point, buyers who align themselves with a buyer's agent as soon as they begin planning a move will be pleasantly surprised that a strategic buyer's agent will not only open doors, but can source off-market properties, find hidden gems in neighborhoods the buyer might not be considering, and know for certain if a property is a "good deal" based on years of home tours.

Buyers have an incredible amount of data at their fingertips, but sorting through it all can be daunting. Agents are tour guides to the most important local details, like fastest commuter routes, hidden parks or recreation areas, and where the best restaurants are. More and more properties come to market without a public listing; don't miss out by just waiting for them to hit the public websites like Zillow or Realtor.com. We partner with our buyers to ensure they have the extra advantage of advanced notice, sometimes a critical factor in their submitting the winning bid.

The housing crisis of 2006-2008 recalibrated the marketplace, but still buyers are often surprised at just how important a lender is during their search. With regulations so much tighter, the lender must be responsive, communicative, and intimately versed in the strengths of their buyer. Buyers are being judged in terms of their financial strengths—should the seller trust that this buyer is qualified and financing will go through? Offers will not be considered without pre-approval or proof of funds in a cash offer. In fact, listing agents will often require this proof prior to any showings.

With must more robust underwriting standards, borrowers are surprised at the level of detail the lenders require and how many questions they ask. Buyers should keep in close contact with their lenders throughout the process. And we caution that a buyer should not apply for any department store credit cards, buy furniture, or pay off a vehicle loan during this phase of the transaction. Even paying off a debt can negatively affect a buyer's credit score thereby putting their home loan in jeopardy.

For our cash buyers, showing proof of funds may appear to be intrusive, but we redact personal information, including account numbers, and demonstrate to the sellers just how qualified they are. "Cash is king" for many sellers in their decision of which buyer to select; however, a buyer may offer cash and then choose to secure a mortgage. With the seller's approval, a "cash offer" may actually be a contract free of the financing contingency. Buyers will still go through the process of obtaining a mortgage, but if anything inhibits the approval by settlement, the buyer assumes the risk and must complete the transaction with a cash purchase. Rules and regulations change from time-to-time, so I recommend any buyer considering this option to review it with their financial and tax advisors well in advance to make sure this strategy will be appropriate based on their individual situation.

When a buyer has selected a home to purchase, as a buyer's agent we will help evaluate the fair market value of the property. We create a detailed market analysis, allowing our buyers to feel certain that they are getting a good value when they craft an offer. This offer, while reflective of buyer wants, should also take into account the seller needs, such as their personal timeline or emotional state. Is a daughter getting married or a job change imminent? Occasionally the seller has other important considerations that may not be apparent in just the home sale. If a buyer takes these factors into account, like offering settlement date flexibility or a rent-back period, the seller may choose it over all others.

Buyers may "win" on something beyond price. Professionalism, presentation, communication, and favorable terms may earn the sellers' favor.

## What Buyers Are Saying

*"Working with the Dana Rice Group was a superb experience from the first phone call to the moment when we sealed the deal on our new home. What's more, the members of the Dana Rice Group have become our friends. We trust their judgement, instincts and thorough knowledge of the Bethesda/Chevy Chase real estate market, where we focused our house search. We moved from San Francisco: a daunting cross-country move. Dana Rice took excellent care of us, shepherding us through the house hunt, spending hours with us over email and phone learning about our needs, getting to know our family and then driving around the streets of neighborhoods of Montgomery County showing us houses she thought we could one day call home. We felt completely taken care of and that has held true to the current day, as we make our new house our home. We recommend the Dana Rice Group without reservation and would work with them again in a heartbeat should we ever need to relocate."*
    – S.B.


*"Where to begin! My husband and I closed on our very first home together today! During settlement Dana asked us if she and her team could have done anything different and we were speechless. The entire process was smooth and even fun! Dana took us out almost every weekend in January (during snow and ice storms) to see different neighborhoods and really understand what was right for our family. The only sad part of us buying our house is we won't get to talk to her everyday! If you're looking for an agent that is thoughtful committed and a DMV expert look no further!"*
    – L.C.

*"The Dana Rice Group has commanding expertise over the many neighborhoods they serve. Not only are they knowledgeable and professional, they are an absolute pleasure to partner with during the emotional experience of buying or selling your largest asset. I find them organized, kind, compassionate, reassuring and just all-around fun! I wouldn't use anyone else.*
 *– J.M.*

## Selecting an Agent

There are thousands of real estate agents for good reason: housing is a basic human necessity. We suggest that selecting an agent should be like the process of dating. Not everyone will be a good match for everyone else. Communication style, trustworthiness, risk tolerance, knowledge of local laws, rules, regulations, not to mention knowledge the real estate inventory overall, are critical in selecting an agent. It's important to pick a partner who not only provides information, but also will be in frequent communications and dedicated to your personal goals. An agent that is the right choice for a neighbor or friend may not be the right choice for another. I recommend that prospective buyers and sellers talk with three or more agents before making a selection. We as agents play a key role in a client's financial affairs over a concentrated period of time, so we encourage them to feel absolutely confident in their choice.

Due to the local focus of real estate, buyers and sellers should determine the agent's knowledge of the market and experience in specific neighborhoods. For a buyer moving from another area of the country, look for a proactive partner who knows the nuances of each neighborhood. This decision can have a major impact on enjoyment of living in the home for years to come.

After strategic pricing, marketing is the most critical in selling for the highest amount in the shortest time. Sellers should inquire how the agent plans to market the property: Does the agent use professional photography and videos? Does she write engaging descriptions? Does he understand what word choice evokes what behavior in the target audience? Is she investing in online exposure, print advertising, and direct mail? Potential buyers for luxury homes will include professionals, business executives, professional athletes, possibly entertainers, and people in politics. How will the agent reach the individuals that are the most likely buyers? Do they have a network of other agents who are equally productive and impactful? Take some time to find the perfect partner in this journey.

## About Dana Rice

Dana Rice (dana.rice@compass.com) is Senior Vice President at Compass in Washington, D.C.

Dana's growth in the Washington, D.C. market has been swift and significant since her real estate career launch in 2013. In just the five years, Dana and her group of top agents have sold more than $150M, and expect an additional $80M in 2018. Dana's team of four full-time agents, transaction coordinator, and dedicated stager, are active in their community, and highly regarded in the DC/MD/VA market.

She specializes in high-value residences between $800k and $2.0M+, focusing on the geographic regions of Northwest D.C., Bethesda and Chevy Chase, Maryland.

Dana also is a real estate investor, owning multiple rental properties. As an activist builder, Dana buys distressed properties for major restoration and renovation. She does not consider herself one who "flips" properties as her efforts are year-long labors of love, with thoughtful design and execution. Dana works with great care to maintain the existing character of the home, the street, and the neighborhood, as these concerns will yield more money for sale or rental. She dramatically enhances size, finishes and overall aesthetic of her properties. There are no "McMansions" in Dana Rice's world… just elegant homes that nestle beautifully into their natural setting.

Dana has been awarded *Washingtonian* Top 100 Agent in DC, Best of Washington, 2015-2018; Compass #1 team in year-over-year growth and Compass Top Ten Producer Awards. Dana is frequently featured in real estate news articles and reports as an expert in the local real estate market.

For more information about Dana Rice, visit http://www.DanaRiceGroup.com.

# Buying and Selling Luxury Homes in Seattle

# Moira E. Holley

## Introduction

Moira Holley started her sales career in luxury goods including fashion and art. During that time she developed a passion for fine home architecture and design. Recognizing that the local luxury real estate community in the '90s needed an agent with a strong sense of design sensibility, Moira made a natural transition into representing buyers and sellers with their luxury property transactions.

Moira is a Co-Founder of Realogics Sotheby's Realty in Seattle where she is a Senior Global Real Estate Advisor. She helps buyers and sellers of luxury residences in the metropolitan and downtown Seattle area including waterfront properties along Lake Washington. Her clients include C-Level executives of Fortune 50 Companies, start-up entrepreneurs, and area professionals.

In this chapter Moira offers insight for buyers and sellers of luxury homes in the Seattle area.

## Selling Your Luxury Home

Homeowners interested in selling their Seattle luxury property should contact an agent at least three months in advance of the planned listing date. Most homes need at least some preparation or could benefit from staging to make them more attractive to potential buyers. Starting discussions with an agent well in advance provides the owner plenty of time to get their home in shape to be shown, which is a critical aspect of getting the most value from the sale.

At the first meeting with an agent, most sellers are interested in knowing what their home is likely to sell for when it is placed on the market. Whereas the market value of average price-range properties can be analyzed using more of a statistical approach with adjustments for differences, most luxury properties are very unique in design and amenities. It takes real understanding of the luxury home market and buyer preferences to determine what a buyer might be willing to pay. These properties require the agent to think more like a high-end appraiser and requires significant skill and years of experience in the market.

Springtime is the busiest home selling season in the Seattle area and we typically have another fairly busy season in the fall. We encourage our clients to list their properties before the spring rush. That way they can take advantage of the year's peak buying season. Another compelling reason for listing in the spring is that you have time for a second marketing push in the fall if for some reason the property doesn't sell quickly. This is particularly relevant for properties over $5 million, which generally do not move as quickly as properties listed at a million or two less.

Here in Seattle, the market can quiet down during the summer months. We have the beautiful San Juan Islands nearby and many of our local buyers—and sellers, too—split their time between their city and island homes, or pass the summer on their boats. Right after Labor Day is another good time to put a property on the market, with the objective of selling before Halloween, because market activity drops precipitously in November and December. The last two months of the year are not a good time to list a single-family residence; it would be better to wait till after the New Year's holiday.

There's not as much seasonality with condominiums. You're in a tower, so buyers don't have to be out in the weather. Buying activity on Seattle-area condominiums holds steady throughout the year, with the exception being the brief period between Thanksgiving and New Year's.

Your home needs to be in "show condition" from the moment it goes on the market. One of the benefits I provide my clients is to walk through the entire home with them and offer a list of things to enhance the salability of their property. Sometimes the property may needs some significant preparation. Even when in very good overall condition I've found that many times there are small details that the owner, through a natural familiarity with the home, has missed. It may be small things that need repairing, like little nicks and scrapes in the stucco, blown seals in the windows, a crack they'd forgotten about in a wall behind a door, or any evidence of settling. Everything needs to appear in very good condition. The gardens on such properties are usually in great shape; but if they're not, then I make recommendations for people who can come in quickly and spruce things up.

I always tell my clients that homes are either designed for living or they're designed for selling—and often these are two very different things. Frequently we'll have a professional home stager come in and evaluate the seller's furniture and its arrangement in the home. It's pretty common to observe crowded spaces and certain pieces visually cutting off rooms. Removing some furniture and changing the arrangement often can maximize the welcoming aspect of the home and make it appear larger. It's generally just editing the amount and placement of furnishings in the home.

De-cluttering is an important and often overlooked aspect of preparing a home for sale. In high-end properties, the clutter—if it exists at all—tends to be comprised of art collections. An overabundance of art can be a distraction for a buyer walking through the home, and can even be a distraction for a buyer viewing photos online. Often buyers get interested in the art and will focus on that instead of the home. That can result in a short memory of the features of the home itself. Just like with the furnishings, we want to edit the art that will be displayed in the home during the selling process.

Once the home is elegantly styled and staged for selling, the time has arrived for a professional photographer to capture the beauty of your property. We like to use a variety of exterior day-and-night images, including some beautiful garden shots taken in the morning, and some twilight shots taken in the evening. We also capture the interior of the home at various times of the day to enable prospective buyers to imagine themselves living there. The importance of using a talented, professional photographer can't be overstated. Unfortunately, a lot of the digital photography we see in home sales today is uninspired, flat, and lifeless, and that's simply not the way to present a luxury property.

Still photography has its limitations, though. The scale of estate properties makes it difficult for simple photographs—no matter how artfully composed—to adequately tell the tale of the property. In such instances

I am more likely to use video. Drone videos offer the viewer a compelling vision of the property and its vicinity: the scale of the house and acreage; the neighborhood in which the house sits; and the layout of the surrounding area. Plus, if your property happens to be in a particularly prestigious neighborhood, with nearby parks and landmarks, video offers an ideal way to tell an expanded story beyond the house.

We live in a visual age. Experience has proven to me that photography and video, and only the best photography and video, is what provokes buyers and holds their interest. We always make sure that the first three photos displayed in the various real estate listings are of the most important features and of the highest quality, because selling a property today is about keeping people's attention. If you lose their attention on the first click, they're gone. But if you can keep their attention through three clicks, then you can be certain they're going to actively engage with the listing. That's why we always want the very best photographs in the first three slots.

Potential buyers of luxury properties here in the Seattle area are located all over the world and not just in our area. Wide exposure to potential buyers, wherever they may currently live, is vital to selling a luxury property. Some methods of exposure may seem obvious, but bear emphasizing, for they're the first line of attack in selling a property. In addition to local multiple listing services, we gain exposure for your property through our luxury global networks. My own listings are uploaded to our local Realogics Sotheby's website, and from there to Sotheby's International Realty global network. The opportunity for international marketing and global reach through Sotheby's is a significant advantage.

Luxury lifestyle magazines are generally published in both print and digital versions, and provide another means of reaching interested and qualified buyers around the world. *Haute Living*, for example, is magazine for high net worth readers in four major cities, but it also has an online version for viewers around the U.S. and the world. *Clientele Luxury*, meanwhile, focuses on real estate and other exclusive products. Real estate brokers can participate in these networks by invitation only, and I'm very honored to be the only real estate broker in the Seattle area—or in the entire state of Washington, for that matter—invited to participate in these networks. I'm also happy to be a contributor to *Fourhundred Luxury Lifestyle Magazine*. These networks have very active social media, so on my posts I'm able to tag the participating networks, which then send my listings to their subscribers. This has been a great platform to get potential buyers to view our luxury listings.

Social media is another great way to gain exposure for home listings. Facebook, and especially Instagram, are the best for exposing real estate. On Instagram, you can load up to 10 images at a time; Instagram stacks the images as a single post, but lets viewers know that there are more than one photograph. Smartphones allow you to swipe through all the photos. An Instagram post can then be shared to Facebook, which helpfully reformats it for that platform, and even keeps the shots in the same order.

Increasingly, the Seattle area attracts a significant number of international buyers. In recent years, most of the interest has come from Asia, and in particular, China. It's important, therefore, to get exposure in the Chinese market. Our brokerage partnered with a local magazine that created a Mandarin-language edition that targets Asian residents of Seattle. It's given out for free at Seattle's highest-visibility tourist attractions. These magazines are also sent to selected locations in Asia and are mailed to ultra high net worth individuals throughout that continent. I regularly place full-page ads in this magazine to feature my luxury listings.

At the bottom of every page in the magazine there's a number to call for readers interested in purchasing a home in the area. We have what we call an "Asia Desk," and the number goes directly to it, where a Mandarin-speaking agent is ready to take the call. That way, we brokers who do not speak Mandarin can sell properties to buyers who would otherwise go unserved. We partner with Mandarin-speaking brokers who can carry the conversation for us, which is helpful for everyone involved. It saves the buyer and the broker from being mutually frustrated by a language barrier.

We also advertise on national real estate websites and utilize email marketing to announce new listings. We typically share our new listings with several thousand brokers. If we're hosting an open house, then we do a lot of email marketing in addition to our standard social media push. The importance of social media use can't be overstated; it keeps you connected to people who already like what you do, and who are always watching your feed.

Once on the market, it's important to make sure the home is kept in show condition every day. This means that it needs to be kept clean and tidy at all times. Even if your listing insists on a 24-hour notice for showings, there inevitably will be a prospective buyer who needs to see your property right away. Maybe they are from out of the area and have a very limited amount of time to see your property. It's always better to accommodate a potential buyer with a showing instead of missing out on an opportunity for a sale.

When working with a seller, the objective is for me to find a buyer and then settle at a price that satisfies that seller. Over time, I've developed a strategy that helps move the transaction in that direction. Generally, when a buyer's agent is preparing to make an offer, they notify the seller's agent. This is a great opportunity for me to prep the buyer, through the buyer's agent, on what the seller is looking for. We can indicate the level of interest from other potential buyers and indicate whether other buyers are circling. We can also express other considerations that would be favorable to the seller, such as a desired closing schedule, or a rent-back provision if the seller needs time to move. In this way, we can be working toward a winning strategy even before the offer is formally presented to the seller and it helps get an initial offer closer to meeting the seller's goals, possibly reducing the counter-offer cycle.

A luxury home is a major asset and a specialized approach is needed to generate the most money out of a sale. Most people of means want to be represented by experts when making significant transactions, and selling your home should not be an exception.

## Buying Your Luxury Home

With all of the online home listings that are common these days, potential buyers sometimes wonder if they need a real estate agent to help them identify and purchase a new home. Although one can see most homes for sale listed online, finding potentially attractive properties is only a small step in the process to successfully purchase a home. It's also important to remember that a seller's agent works for the seller, has a fiduciary responsibility to the seller, and represents the seller in the negotiations. On the other hand a buyer's agent represents the buyer and works on behalf of the buyer in negotiations and navigating all through the home buying process.

Online listings are not always up-to-date, and not all available homes are listed online. A buyer's agent will have access to the most up-to-date listings and an experienced luxury agent may even have access to listings otherwise private and publicly unavailable. For buyers moving into the area, an experienced agent can guide them toward locations or neighborhoods that will best fit their needs. They may even have seen specific homes through two or three selling cycles. This allows them to know the fabric and nuances of neighborhoods in way that eludes the average buyer searching alone on the Internet.

Since your agent is there to provide optimal assistance in finding the locations and neighborhoods that will best meet your needs, you should be as open as possible—and as specific as possible—about your objectives. I like to have an initial conversation with prospective buyers to get to know their preferences, goals, and personality to better understand the life they'll be building in the house I've been tasked with helping them find.

There are, of course, many considerations to keep in mind when searching for a home. What type of lifestyle are you looking for? What kinds of neighborhood amenities are important? Do you prefer an urban vibe, or are you more interested in a suburban location? Do you love the thought of living within walking distance of cafes and coffeehouses, or do you want something more secluded? Do you prefer the countryside, or do you want waterfront views? How long do you plan to be in the new home? Are you interested in creating a home and stay there for many years? Or do you instead prefer to try something new for a while and then move a few years later?

If you have a family, then schools will likely be a key consideration. I try to determine the most important factors in my clients' desire for their children's education. For example, Seattle has many schools known for excelling in certain disciplines. Do the parents want a neighborhood where the school focuses on a specific subject—math, for example, or the arts? Or do they want their children attending one of the wonderful public schools? Preferences for education opportunities will focus the search for areas and neighborhoods that will best meet their needs.

Establishing a budget for the new home will be a key factor in determining locations that will work for the buyer. If mortgage financing will be used for part of the purchase price, it's critical to start working with a lender and get a pre-approval letter, even before starting the home search. I have relationships with local lenders and mortgage brokers who do a great job in underwriting, and can help buyers get a very clear picture of their ability to secure financing. In today's market, sellers and their agent will generally not consider any offers unless there is clear documentation of the buyer's ability to fund the purchase. They don't want to take their home off the market and then find out later that the buyer is not able to follow through with the purchase. All-cash purchases are pretty common on high-end properties, and proof of funds will be required as evidence. If mortgage financing will be used, a pre-approval letter will be required. Occasionally, sellers and their agents will even require proof of funds or pre-approval before showing a property. Owners of luxury properties only want serious buyers getting a look inside their homes and don't want their time wasted with showings to unqualified buyers.

Often, buyers are quite capable of paying in cash, but for tax or other purposes they prefer to use a mortgage for part for the purchase price. In a competitive situation, a buyer might make an offer without a financing contingency but let the seller know the buyer intends to get a loan for part of the purchase price. Proof of funds and a reasonable amount of earnest money keeps a seller's mind at ease in this type of situation.

After understanding a buyer's goals and budget, it's time to visit neighborhoods and individual properties that are most likely to meet their objectives. As we are helping buyers narrow down the alternatives, we also help them understand the tradeoffs of the properties being considered. Finally, before making an offer we provide an analysis of the market value. This is pretty similar to an analysis we perform for sellers. Often we will reach out to the listing agent to understand their pricing rationale and find out which comparable properties they used in arriving at a price. This information can be beneficial in getting a better idea if a price is justified. At the same time we gather as much insight as possible on terms that may be important to the seller.

When structuring an offer, it's important to understand that price, while always important, is not always the only factor that plays a role in meeting the seller's objectives. Knowing the seller's goals in advance helps us craft an informed offer that may be able to satisfy the seller on terms other than just matching the listing price. Sometimes the closing date or a short-term rent back is important to a seller and by accommodating on such needs we can possible get a lower price offer accepted.

Once we have negotiated an offer and it's been accepted, a contingency period begins in which the buyer takes several steps to inspect the property being purchased. The time for inspections to be completed is negotiated in the agreement, but in this area it's generally a week or less, so prompt action is necessary to get inspections completed. If it's a single-family home, then a thorough home inspection should be completed. In my experience, the foundation and the sewer line are the two most important areas to investigate. A sewer scope expert should be hired to check for breaks or tree root problems in the line. The foundation should be checked for any slippage. A general home inspection will also include checking the roof, gutters, windows, drainage on site, and the mechanical systems. If indications of issues are discovered, we will suggest bringing in specialists for further investigation and estimates of cost to mitigate the issues. Discovery of significant issues generally calls for further negotiation on terms that might include having the seller get repairs completed or a reduction in price. Unfavorable findings will generally allow a buyer to walk away from the purchase and receive a return of the earnest money deposited.

Condominium properties are much easier properties to shuttle through the contingency process. In Washington, the legislature passed the Condominium Act, which mandates a five-day period to review the re-sale certificate, the declarations, the budget, the reserves (to get an idea of the financial condition of the association), CC&Rs, as well as the homeowner association's meeting minutes. The meeting minutes are very helpful for buyers to understand how well the owners get along with each other in managing the association and can catch a glimpse of life in the building and decide if they want to share in it.

Purchasing a home is a major financial investment and having an experienced luxury agent working on your side to navigate you through the process and handle the negotiations will give you peace of mind and help you make the best decision for you situation.

## Selecting the Best Agent for You

The best way to start your search for an agent is to ask for personal recommendations from friends. Have any of them had a great experience buying or selling with a particular broker? Listen to their stories and ask who they've worked with. Then go online to the recommended agent's website and look around. Find out why they're in real estate. Look at the kinds of properties they're presenting on their website and watch a video walk-through of one of them. Are your tastes aligned? Do you see things that excite you? Look at online testimonials. In general, see if this agent a good fit.

If you're selling, find an agent who knows your area. If you're in neighborhood where homes sell frequently, find out who the neighborhood experts are. A neighborhood expert can give you solid advice based on experience in that neighborhood. They probably know from week-to-week and month-to-month what the market is doing in your specific area. Look for an agent's transaction volume of luxury properties, as this is usually a very good indicator of whether they're well experienced in higher-end home transactions.

At its heart, this business is all about relationships. In the coming weeks and months, you're going to be spending a good deal of time with an agent who will accompany you in selling your property or in the pursuit of your dream home. It's therefore important to find an agent whose company you enjoy and whose judgment you trust.

## What Clients Are Saying

"Moira and her team have listed and sold two separate homes for us in Seattle over the pat year. The level of professionalism and expertise exhibited were of an extraordinary level. We have been involved in more than 10 real estate transactions in the past decade or so (both buying and selling) and no other real estate team has come close to matching the high level of quality that was realized in working with Moira's team. I would recommend her without hesitation."

    - dnagle1

"Moira's reputation precedes her when it comes to downtown loft spaces & luxury properties. My sale is a perfect example of what can happen when you choose the right agent for the right property. When I decided to list, I asked Moira to represent me based on recommendations from her previous clients. I sent an email to Moira via her website. Within minutes, I received my first phone call and we met at my property the following day. I immediately felt comfortable with her knowledge of how we should position the property & her pricing strategy. I left for a vacation to allow her to work her magic & hold an open house. Within 10 days of listing, we had multiple strong offers.

"Moira also represented me in securing a new property within Seattle. It was like a melding of minds when we discussed the type of property I wanted to purchase. She immediately knew what I was looking for and didn't waste my time with properties that didn't fit within that description. She was also great at allowing me to proceed *at my own pace as I went through mortgage underwriting. When it came time to make an offer on the property I wanted, we were up against competing offers. Her strategies for writing the offer & the speed with which she executed was the difference between getting the property I wanted & continuing to look (and having to make other living arrangements between the two closing processes - HUGE deal). I couldn't ask for a more professional agent or a smoother process. Absolutely awesome."*

    - rainydaze999

*"Moira has helped us sell two condos in N Seattle (Fremont and Ballard) in the past five years. Our last sale was completed and closed 17 days after listing the property. She helps you get your property ready for listing (staging, painting) and she works with you to set the right price for the property to attract buyers while maximizing your proceeds."*

    - user 6830382

*"In depth knowledge of Seattle's luxury residential market and neighborhoods. Fully transparent. Great broker relationships, so she knows both what is on the market, what is likely to come to market, and has all the details on comparable transactions."*

    - user 85902038

*"If you are attempting to find a premium property in the Seattle area, then you should look no further than Moira Holley's website. There you will find her collection of the most exquisite homes in Seattle. After perusing this impressive portfolio of uniquely "hand-*

*picked" design-savvy residences, you will see that Moira has most certainly reached the pinnacle of her profession.*

*"Elegantly casual - yet a consummate professional - she will make the diverse choices of Seattle neighborhoods a pleasurable adventure with her magical sense of effortlessly producing just exactly what you are seeking.*

*"Moira's inside knowledge of what is a "good buy" that week is an acquired talent obviously and impressive. Hopefully, as with our experience, she will continue guiding new clients happily into their next new home with the same flair and solid advice."*
- user 9595652

*"Moira and her team did an amazing job handling the entire sale of my unit. I'd given them a tough job - refurbishing, staging, and listing a unit that I had been renting out, all while I was living remotely 800 miles away.*

*"I was worried about how difficult it was going to be to sell my property, especially because I was currently remote, but Moira made it a breeze every step of the way. Everyone involved was professional, efficient, had fantastic market expertise, and provided extremely good advice for everything from refurbishing to pricing.*

*"My unit sold quickly and for a price that I was very satisfied with, and I'd recommend Moira and her team to anyone looking for a real estate agent in the Seattle area."*
- user 5454984

## About Moira E. Holley

Moira Holley is a Co-Founder of Realogics Sotheby's Realty in Seattle where she is a Senior Global Real Estate Advisor. She has been ranked as the leading Broker for all brokerages of Realogics Sotheby's nearly every year, since 2010 and is consistently listed among the top 1% of the Northwest's leading luxury real estate professionals. Moira was selected for membership in Sotheby's Market Leaders Forum, an invitation-only forum made up of 45 of Sotheby's International Realty's top United States brokers.

Moira represents buyers and sellers of luxury single family and condominium residences in the metropolitan and downtown Seattle area including waterfront properties along Lake Washington. Her clients include C-Level executives of Fortune 50 Companies, start-up entrepreneurs, and area professionals.

Moira is frequently featured by local and national news media as an expert on trends in luxury real estate. Her analysis has been featured in *The Wall Street Journal*, *The Puget Sound Business Journal*, and other leading business, professional, and real estate sector-specific publications.

Moira is a strong supporter of a number of the Northwest's most respected community service organizations, including Mary's Place, the Film School, The Seattle Art Museum, the Olympic Sculpture Park, The Seattle Humane Society, The DT Fleming Arboretum, and the Evergreen Golden Retriever Rescue.

For more information about Moira Holley, visit www.MoiraPresents.com.

# Buying and Selling Luxury Homes in Highlands and Cashiers, NC

# Liz Harris

## Introduction

Liz Harris has been affiliated with McKee Properties in Cashiers, North Carolina since 2004 where she is a broker and partner in the firm. Liz specializes in fine estates and homes in Cashiers and Highlands, NC as well as the area's golf club communities like Wade Hampton Golf Club, Mountaintop Golf and Lake Club, and The Chattooga Club.

Liz got her start in the real estate industry by building and selling a home in the Cashiers area. She has always been interested in land and homes, so real estate became her passion. In addition to helping buyers and sellers in the Highlands and Cashiers area, she has personally been involved in building and selling 6 homes of her own.

In this chapter Liz provides her insights for luxury home buyers and sellers in the Highlands and Cashiers area of western North Carolina. The Highlands/Cashiers plateau at around a 4,000-foot elevation is a popular second home destination for people who want to escape the summertime heat of the cities.

## Selling Your Luxury Home

Luxury properties are always unique, and there is an art to analyzing and estimating a market value. A comparative market analysis, or CMA, is always a good place to start. A competitive market analysis looks at recent sales prices of comparable properties, making adjustments for differences between the home being analyzed and the other properties. I also use cost replacement as another indicator of value. This method considers the land value plus the cost to construct all of the components of the home. Cost replacement value per square foot varies by the type of space, so different costs are associated with heated and unheated space on the main level, lower level, and upper level as well as for porches, decks, a garage, and other additional home structures. If the house is older, we also factor in a deduction for depreciation. Buyers like to see this type of analysis because it provides an objective and logical viewpoint on value. Sometimes a seller will get an official appraisal to help with value assessment. Having an appraisal upfront is something that buyers appreciate, and it can add to the credibility of a listing price.

Current competition on the market is another factor for pricing. Think in terms of the properties a buyer is going to be looking at in a similar price range and how those other properties on the market compare to your property.

Pricing a home also depends on the market conditions, such as the level of inventory and number of sales being made in a year in a similar price range. The seller's motivation level is also a critical component of pricing. A seller who isn't in a hurry to sell may be able to wait for the right buyer to come along and offer a favorable price. If a seller is motivated to sell, the price should definitely be below the competing properties as there are only a certain number of homes that sell in each price range in a given year.

Like most luxury home markets, many of the homes in the area are custom-built, or the owners have made customized improvements to their homes. Sellers shouldn't typically expect to get the dollars back out of customizations when it's time to sell. It's important to understand that tastes differ among people, and something attractive to one person may not be desired by all. Bright colors on the walls, very artistic tiles, and other special finishings could be viewed by some buyers as features that need to be changed, so they may actually deduct value for a feature they don't like. There may be a beautiful built-in hot tub, but not all buyers want a hot tub. Some may consider it a hassle and figure they'll have to pay to have it removed. These are just some examples of features that are for enjoyment during ownership, but you can't expect everyone to appreciate them at the same level.

When we're putting a home on the market, presentation is a big key for success. The home should look freshly painted and well kept. When preparing for sale, I walk through a home and make a thorough list of recommendations on maintenance items to be taken care of as well as cosmetic changes to freshen up the home. Sometimes I suggest furniture rearrangement and other staging that will open the home up and make it show better.

Most of the owners in the area are not full-time residents, so keeping the exterior of the home in good showing order is something to consider while the home is on the market. Many owners have a home caretaker who comes by every week and checks on the landscaping to make sure that anything needing attention gets handled.

Often sellers don't want to spend money on a home they are leaving, but they need to keep in mind what a buyer's view of the home might be if there are some major maintenance issues such as a need for painting or a roof that is failing. If there is $10,000 of work needed to repair something obvious to potential buyers, they will probably discount the value by $50,000 in their minds. Sellers who don't want to repair this type of problem will probably end up paying much more in price reductions than in spending the money on the repairs upfront. It's also important after a home is on the market to listen to feedback from people who have viewed the home. Feedback provides clues as to why a home may not be selling. Sometimes it is something simple that can be changed or adjusted to make it more attractive.

The best time to put a home on the market in our area is March or April. That way you catch people who are interested in buying a home before the summer season begins. Unfortunately, outdoor photography is not great at this time because the leaves haven't come out on the trees yet, so we'll come back a little later and get new outdoor photos. The area is becoming more of a year-round destination, which is attracting winter buyers as well. So if you really want every chance possible to sell your home, it can be listed at any time of the year.

After the home is prepared for listing, we capture its beauty with a series of professional photos and videos to be used for marketing. Most potential buyers are going to be seeing your home for the first time while looking online, so we want excellent photography to attract their attention and get them interested in personally seeing the home. Professional photography that shows the home in attractive lighting and from the best angles is critical to showcasing the home. We typically select 20 to 30 photos to place in our online listings. Videos help viewers envision the flow of the home, especially for larger homes. We are also now using aerial videos to show the view and setting of the home as well as nearby amenities.

Exposure of your home to the most potential buyers is a key to selling your home for the most money and in the shortest time. Buyers in the Highlands/Cashiers area are primarily coming from the southeastern United States, Texas, Louisiana, Tennessee, Oklahoma, and many states within a day's drive of us, although we do have some buyers who live in other areas, including the Northeast and the West Coast. Online advertising is probably the most important way for buyers to find a home in today's market, especially since most of our buyers are not in the area. Our agency listings are widely distributed online to a number of premium real estate listing sites. Additionally, we own the Cashiers.com website, which is a popular site for all of the events happening around Cashiers. Our agency listings are highlighted on this site. Promoting the wonderful lifestyle this area provides is key to selling real estate.

We also use print advertising to expose a property. For example, we advertise in a local magazine, "The Laurel," which is on display in all of the hotels in the area. We also advertise luxury listings in other magazines in targeted cities as well as in national magazines.

Personally, my success is through direct marketing and relationships. Our agency is over 40 years old, and we have gathered an extensive mailing list of past, present, and prospective clients. We have a newsletter that is emailed to thousands of people on our list every week, showcasing our listings. Most important though are the relationships I cultivate in simple ways every day and in more extravagant ways through local events.

Selling a home in this market is different than selling in a city. People interested in buying a second home are in a more relaxed frame of mind, and there's no rush to buy. They tend to go back home after viewing properties, think about it a while, and maybe come back a few times before making a decision. So the time frame for selling these homes is substantially longer than in a city.

## Buying Your Luxury Home

The Highlands/Cashiers plateau is in the western North Carolina mountains, near the border with Georgia and South Carolina. We're within a day's drive from a third of the United States population. The area has become known as a second home destination. At around 4,000-foot elevation in the mountains, it's 10 to 20 degrees cooler in the summer than the cities in the Southeast. Highlands and Cashiers are both cute small mountain towns with lots of shopping and dining as well as calendars full of events all summer long. Highlands has been widely described as the "Aspen of the East."

The plateau is an outdoor-lovers paradise. There are 13 golf clubs, including one consistently ranked by "Golf Digest" among America's Top 100 Golf Courses. Other outdoor activities include hiking, mountain and road biking, fishing, and rock climbing. The mountain scenery is beautiful with lots of lakes and waterfalls, and some of the best fall color displays in the East. With moderate summer temperatures and fresh air, the area is a great escape from the cities of the Southeast.

When considering a location for a home in the area, think about how you want to spend your vacation time. Some people may like to be right in one of the towns, close to shopping and dining. Many of our buyers enjoy golf and want to be in a country club community with all of the amenities of a club. That's a great choice for people who want to make friends and have a full calendar of activities to enjoy. The clubs have concierge services to help make arrangements for outings, picnics, planning parties, and other events.

Other buyers want to be in a peaceful environment in nature away from town. If you enjoy fishing, there are a number of lakeside communities that might be a good choice. We've had some people move initially to a country club community and after a few years are very comfortable with the extended area. They might decide to buy more acreage and move to a small farm or estate in the area while maintaining their club membership.

When a buyer has selected a community and a specific property of interest, I'll help the buyer make an informed decision on pricing. Generally several homes in a similar price range have been viewed, so that is one reference point. Just like when working with a seller, we will review recent sales of as many similar homes as possible to analyze a value based on comparable sales. Another contributing piece of data is the percentage of properties that are selling off of listing price. I've also found that buyers are better informed if we complete an estimate of replacement cost — the value of the land and the cost to construct a similar home, less depreciation. Considering the value from different angles helps narrow down the best estimate of a fair market value.

After an offer is negotiated and agreed upon, buyers will have time to carry out inspections and other studies to ensure they are informed on specifically what they are buying. The North Carolina standard contract form is very buyer-friendly with a due diligence period. The specific amount of time for due diligence is whatever the buyer and seller agree upon, but it's typically around 30 days. During this due diligence period, buyers have the option to perform any kind of inspections or tests they want. Typical inspections that buyers would have performed include a general home inspection, a pest inspection, and a radon test. If issues are found with any of the mechanical systems, a specialist might also be brought in to check the equipment.

If the property is outside the towns or golf club communities, a well and septic system may serve the home. In this case, the well and septic system should be inspected to make sure everything is in good working order. If the buyer is planning on remodeling the home, this is also a time to bring in a builder and get some estimates. If purchasing a raw lot, buyers typically at least get an estimate on the cost of a driveway and foundations that might affect the overall construction cost of a new home. If the home purchase is subject to financing approval, the lender approval will need to be finalized during the due diligence period.

Because of the nature of the area as a second home destination, there are a number of home management services available to look around your home to make sure everything is okay while you are away. If they see any issues, they will inform the owner, and if a contractor or other service provider is necessary to remedy any problems, they will gather estimates and manage the entire process. Service after the sale is important to me as well. I'm generally the first person that my buyers will call after the purchase to get familiar with options in the area for service providers.

## How to Choose the Best Agent for You

Buying or selling a home requires a lot of communication and time working with an agent to accomplish your goals, so it's important to pick an agent you can enjoy working with all the way through completion of the process. This is one of the most significant transactions in life, so you want to make sure that you are dealing with a person who is well-experienced and can be trusted to look out for your interests. I would also suggest looking at the experience and reputation of the company behind the agent. Firsthand experience in buying and selling properties of their own is another trait that indicates personal knowledge and experience.

If you are selling your home, ask to review the marketing the agent has done for other similar properties in the area. Is the agent willing to spend on a variety of marketing strategies to expose your home to potential buyers? Past success is important as successful agents have more of an ability to spend on marketing your home.

If you're thinking of buying, make sure the agent is knowledgeable of the different locations and can help guide you to a place you can enjoy for the long term as well as be able to sell down the road. Many of our buyers have an interest in purchasing in a country club community, so access to several of the clubs where they can enjoy golfing and dining out is going to be key to helping them make a decision about which property to invest in.

## What Clients Are Saying

*"Liz Harris was a pleasure to work with. Very knowledgeable and experienced in the Cashiers and Highlands market. Having personally and successfully bought and sold, built and remodeled homes in the area, she offers more expertise than most. She understood our ultimate goal for a home and lifestyle in the area and found exactly what we were looking for."*

*"Liz was wonderful to work with. She clearly cared about the long term satisfaction of us and our purchase in Cashiers. Her knowledgeable about the area and personal experience with successful buying and selling was comforting and very helpful."*

## About Liz Harris

Liz Harris is a partner of McKee Properties and is one of the Highlands and Cashiers area's top real estate brokers. She has been affiliated with McKee Properties since 2004 and was fortunate to have been mentored by the firm's founder, the late A. William McKee.

Liz specializes in fine estates and homes in Cashiers and Highlands as well as in the area's premier golf club communities including Wade Hampton Golf Club,

Mountaintop Golf and Lake Club, and The Chattooga Club. She has been a partner in a number of successful real estate projects and investments in the Cashiers area. Liz also provides her clients direct access to development and construction consultation. Her knowledge of the broad range of communities and properties in the Highlands and Cashiers area helps buyers narrow their search to the right property. Her experience in these communities and her large network of potential buyers helps sellers effectively market and sell their properties.

For more information about Liz Harris and McKee Properties, visit http://www.McKeeProperties.com/Meet-Your-Agent/Liz-Harris

# Buying and Selling Luxury Homes in Park City, Utah

# Nancy Tallman

## Introduction

Nancy Tallman began her sales and negotiation career in California in the health care industry where she negotiated multi-million dollar contracts between physician groups, hospitals, and insurance companies. She and her husband relocated to Park City in 2003. After relocating, Nancy decided to pursue her passion for real estate, and at the same time, her dream of owning her own business.

Nancy is affiliated with Summit Sotheby's International Realty in Park City, Utah, where she has helped hundreds of clients buy and sell their homes in the area. Over 65% of her business comes from referrals and repeat clients. An active booster of the Park City community, Nancy writes a weekly real estate blog at insideparkcity.com, with thousands of readers throughout the United Stares.

In this chapter Nancy provides the reader insights for buying and selling luxury homes in Park City, Utah, one of the leading ski and year-round recreational resort communities in the United States.

## Selling Your Luxury Home

When planning on selling your home, the best place to start is to organize objectives for the sale. Pricing and timing are generally the top considerations. Most homeowners I work with have a pretty good idea about value; however, an analysis of comparable sales by an experienced agent with local knowledge is always recommended. As we move up in price range, we are dealing with custom homes that are unique in many aspects related to value. Examples include size of the home and lot, construction quality, the view, level of finishes, age, and condition. In a resort community like Park City, value is also based on proximity to amenities, such as skiing, golfing, or a clubhouse. Direct ski-out access to the lifts can be a big factor as well as the view.

When establishing a price, setting it competitively is going to make a big difference in the time it will take to sell as well as being able to get the highest price. Buyers and their agents are well informed on statistics and will know if a home is over priced. A home can get great exposure, the best marketing, and have hundreds of showings, but if it's not priced properly, it will linger on the market for a long time. Buyers in the luxury price range generally don't have an urgency to buy and don't expect to be paying higher than market price.

I recommend my clients start preparing their home for sale at least three months prior to listing, so that the home can be properly prepared and we can complete pre-marketing activities. A key goal is to make your home stand out among the competitive homes on the market. I do a detailed walk through of my clients' homes and provide a checklist of steps that should be taken to enhance the market value and shorten the time on the market. It's critical to make sure that the home is in pristine condition and looks as if has been well maintained and that everything is in good working order prior to putting the home on the market. Repair anything that is damaged. Any issues will need to be disclosed and it's better to have repairs completed before the home is on the market. I suggest having a pre-inspection done to uncover any issues that may not be obvious, but that will be discovered during a buyer's inspection in the contingency period after a contract is signed. This allows my clients to take care of repairs according to their own timeline and not during the heat of a negotiation.

An important strategy is depersonalizing and decluttering the home to prepare it for market. I view the process of preparing for sale as making it feel as much as possible like a model home, or a beautiful hotel lobby. Potential buyers can walk in, see a home that is beautifully decorated, but not too specific to a personality. An abundance of personal items and artwork can distract potential buyers from actually seeing the home during a showing, or turn buyers off when they are looking at online photographs.

Staging can make a home attractive to the highest number of buyers and buyers will pay more for homes that are well presented. Some furnishing may be removed or rearranged to open up rooms, views, and lines of sight. With less clutter, it's easier for potential buyers to imagine themselves living in the home. This is important, not just for in-person showings, but in photographs viewed online as well. I include a complementary consultation with a professional local staging company for all my seller clients. If a home is already furnished, most home stagers will be compensated on an hourly basis to carry out the staging activity. Vacant homes do not present as well as beautifully furnished homes, so I always recommend staging for empty homes. Virtual staging is a new cutting edge strategy where furniture is inserted into the photographs of an empty home.

Professional photography is an important aspect of marketing your home and occurs once the home is "show-ready." The first showing is almost always online as that is where most buyers begin looking for a home. We want online photos to not only be of high quality, but to also engage a buyer on an emotional level. The goal is to attract attention so the buyer will click through the photo tour and make an appointment to view the home. Shooting architectural photography is a very specialized skill that most real estate agents do not, themselves, possess. Summit Sotheby's International Realty is unique in that it employs professional photographers who are part of our staff. I meet the photographer at the home to make sure we capture all of the special features of the home that we will be emphasizing in the marketing plan.

I've learned through experience that some homes may require more than one time of day for photos. The inside of the house may look its best at one time of the day, but then to get the best photos of the outside and of the views, we have to shoot at a different time. This is especially true with homes that have a view to the south. We may have to come back either early in the morning, or at the end of the day to be able to take photos of the view. We also like to take twilight photos of the home's exterior to really make it pop.

Depending on the property, we may also use drone photography or videos. With a drone we can get a nice view of the house from above, and see the view in the distance as well. This is especially useful if the property is on a large piece of land or backs up to open space. The viewer can get a bird's-eye view of the whole property and its setting. Video tours are also important for marketing a luxury home and can really capture the "essence" of the home.

After your home has been prepared for sale and we have the photography completed and edited, we are ready for the listing to go live. I select the most visually rich photos of important highlights to go first in the online listings as we only have a few seconds to attract a buyer's attention online. The description and headline for the listing are also critical. Although it seems obvious, attention to detail and avoidance of typos is imperative. Park City homebuyers may be local, reside in other states, or may live in other countries, so wide geographic exposure is imperative, especially in the higher price points. Our listings at Summit Sotheby's International Realty are listed on Sotheby's Realty, which is the most heavily trafficked luxury website and Luxury Real Estate, which is the website with the most luxury properties listed. Our listings are also syndicated to over 5,000 websites around the United States and the world.

You want your home to be seen in places luxury homebuyers frequent. Print media specializing in luxury goods and homes are also a good place to advertise luxury homes in Park City. Magazines like *duPont Registry* and *Unique Homes* are some examples and at Summit Sotheby's International Realty, we have access to advertise in the Sotheby's auction house magazine. Some of these magazines have online versions as well as print versions, so online exposure is enhanced.

Your luxury home in Park City is a major financial asset and there are several key points to getting the highest price and selling in the shortest time. Working with an experienced local agent can make the entire process smoother and maximize the ability to achieve the best outcome for you in the transaction.

## What Sellers Are Saying

*"The sales price you negotiated for our home set a record in our subdivision. It's refreshing to be represented by a realtor with the level of integrity you bring to the table"*
  - Ray K.

*"Nancy was on top of every detail. We felt so pampered by her availability and constant communications with us. She made selling our home both profitable and pleasurable."*
  - Shelby F.

*"I would definitely recommend Nancy to others. She went far beyond the usual level of service and helped me present my home in the best possible light. My friends remarked that the place looked like a magazine show home."*
  - Miki L.

## Buying Your Luxury Home

Many Park City homebuyers are people who have vacationed in Park City, have fallen in love with the town, and decide to move here full time or purchase a vacation home. One of the first steps in searching for a home is to be as clear as possible on what you are looking for as a buyer. Establishing a budget is always a major consideration. Your lifestyle expectations will be important, especially in a resort location like Park City. When a prospective buyer contacts me for the first time, I like to start with a discussion of what is important to them. What do they like to do when they're here? Are they skiers? We have two ski resorts, so if they are familiar with the area, which resort do they prefer? Do they want ski-out access from the home? Are they golfers? Are they interested in a country club setting? Where do they like to eat? Is the view of major importance? Do they plan to be full-time residents or is this a second or third home? If they plan on being part-time residents, are they interested in generating rental income while they are away? Understanding the answers to these questions helps me figure out which neighborhoods are going to be the best fit for them.

In today's age of technology, most home listings can be found online and that is where most buyers start looking for a home. Potential buyers often wonder if they need their own agent or if they should just call the listing agent to view a home. In reality, looking for homes online is a very small first step in purchasing a home. Purchasing a home is a major financial transaction and buyers are well served by having their own agent who will look out for their best interests and help navigate them through the entire process. Many people have a misunderstanding that by working directly with the seller's listing agent, a buyer can save money on the transaction. This is not true and, and in fact, the seller's agent has a fiduciary responsibility to the seller.

An experienced buyer's agent will help you make the best possible deal on a property that best meets your needs.

You may have ruled out properties that didn't present well online, but an experienced local agent may understand that some of these properties would be a good fit. Local agents also may have knowledge of homes that are not yet on market.

After understanding all your goals in purchasing a home, I'll arrange a list of homes that seem to best match what you are looking for. The list will likely include specific properties you have found online as well as others that I believe will match your criteria. I like dividing the home search into a two-day process. We will visit a lot of homes on the first day and help you rank the ones we have looked at. On the second day we will go back with fresh eyes for a more thorough look at the top few candidates. This allows buyers to feel comfortable they have "seen everything" and gives them the time needed to focus on the details of their top choices.

Negotiations are part of every transaction. Price and terms may just be the beginning. Resolution to any issues that arise during the inspection and appraisal process can mean the difference in whether or not the sale proceeds. Vendors, like inspectors and contractors, will be important to assess the condition of a home and its systems. Experienced agents have a list of trusted specialists who can advise on indicated issues.

For the best outcome, it's important to select one buyer's agent who you can trust and stick with that agent. Some people think they can get better results by working with two different agents, but that's not true. All agents have access to the same listings on the MLS. Good agents are networked with each other and learn about new listings before they hit the market. Agents will share their knowledge of the best deals and listings coming to the market in the future with their loyal clients. Of course, if for some reason your relationship with the agent is not working out, you can always work with the broker to switch agents.

As you are starting your home search, I recommend that you clarify your budget and how you will be paying for the home. Most sellers want to know that the buyer has the financial ability to complete the transaction. If mortgage financing will be used, you should be pre-approved, or at least pre-qualified. If you don't already have financing lined up, I have access to very reliable lenders who can complete a thorough pre-approval and will ensure the loan is approved in accordance with the contract deadlines.

If you are using cash for your purchase, the seller will request "proof of funds" to close the transaction. This can be as simple as a bank or brokerage account statement with personal information blacked out. Alternatively, a letter from your financial advisor with pertinent information about liquid assets will be satisfactory.

When you find the home that you are interested in buying, I'll help you structure a realistic offer that not only considers your best interests, but one that is likely to be compelling to a seller. If the property is priced fairly you may need to offer near or at the asking price. If the property is overpriced, there will be room for some negotiations to reach a fair price.

It's very simple to purchase a property in Utah. The standard contract form tends to be skewed toward buyer protections. Contracts usually provide for a 14-day period for the buyer to perform all inspections and other due diligence. Closing is usually set at between 30 and 40 days, during which the financing and appraisal contingencies are removed. Typically we will conduct inspections to determine the physical condition of the structure including the roof, walls, and foundation, as well as the plumbing, electrical, mechanical, and heating and air conditioning systems. This is also the time to verify the location of property lines, acreage of the land and square footage of the home, fees for services such as HOA dues, municipal services, and utility costs. We will also verify any other matters that are material to the buyer in making a decision to purchase the property.

Contingencies are included in the contract to make sure the buyer can make an informed decision about the property and also to provide the seller with the opportunity to correct any major problems that are discovered. Contingencies are not included within the purchase contract to open up an additional avenue to renegotiate the purchase price.

In Utah we use title companies that have escrow officers to facilitate the closing. It's a streamlined process, and lawyers are not involved unless the buyer or seller wants them to be involved. From a buyer's standpoint, there are very few closing costs, aside from the price of the house and the cost of inspections and appraisals. The deed is transferred to your name at the closing. The closing can be in Park City or any other location convenient for the buyer. Many of our buyers do not reside here, so closings frequently are done through the mail using overnight services or by email.

There is a good rental market in Park City and it is a popular resort for investment in rental properties. Some neighborhoods allow listing rentals on sites like AirBNB and there are many property management companies who manage and market rentals. Our resorts and Chamber of Commerce also do a great job in marketing Park City as a destination.

It is critical to understand your objectives when investing in rental properties. The reality in Park City is that you will not achieve positive cash flow if you put down around 20% and finance the balance. However, if you are looking to buy a vacation home and perhaps be able to offset taxes and HOA costs while you are not using it, there are many great options in Park City. Some of our luxury condominiums are the best performing investment properties.

## What Buyers Are Saying

*"Nancy is truly a real estate strategist, committed to meeting her client's needs and executing deals in their best interest. Nancy has a deep knowledge of her market that allows her to write very effective contracts. She is an excellent negotiator. I was especially impressed with how Nancy leverages technology to access market data and speed transactions to closure. We feel lucky to have worked with her."*
   - Chris J.

*"Working with Nancy was a pleasure. I made my requirements clear, Nancy listened to them, showed me properties that matched my requirements and helped me to make a good decision. We closed within a month on my property, and it was an extremely stress free transaction, mainly due to Nancy going above and beyond — and keeping me regularly informed every step of the way."*
   - Terri D.

*"Nancy helped my husband and I find the perfect home in Park City. Since we were new to the area, she gave us valuable information about the neighborhoods, showed us properties that met our criteria and handled our home buying negotiations with integrity and assertiveness. We have lived all over the country and found our home buying experience with Nancy the best!"*

*"I have stayed in contact with her as a trusted real estate professional. She stays on top of the latest real estate trends and statistics in our area and provided us with valuable information. Thanks Nancy!!!"*
   - Kimberly S.

## Selecting the Right Agent for You

Selecting the best agent for your situation is a key to guiding you to a successful conclusion to either buying or selling a home. A luxury home is a valuable investment and selecting an expert to help you thorough the process is just as important as hiring an expert in other fields such as tax, accounting, legal, or medical. You'll be working closely with an agent, so make sure that you have a compatible personality and feel that you can build a relationship based on mutual trust and loyalty. Referrals from friends that have had good experiences are one of the best ways to find an agent. After a referral, do a little research online. In this way you can get a good idea of the agent's specialization and how they market homes. If you don't have any agent referrals, you can search online for luxury home specialists in the area.

The importance of local knowledge and expertise cannot be overstated. Intimate knowledge of comparable properties that have recently sold as well as competitive listings is crucial in getting the best picture of a home's value. Websites that display home listings also provide lists of agents; however, be aware that agents pay to be listed on those sites and just because their name shows up, it doesn't mean that they are local to your area of interest. As an example, I have observed many agents located in Salt Lake City who advertise on these sites as Park City agents. They know the values are typically much higher in Park City and are interested in representing buyers interested in a Park City home. The problem is that they lack local expertise. They do not know the location of trails, public transportation and schools, or vital community information.

Using a true local agent is also important because of the relationships agents have with other local agents. Many agents in our area put out an announcement about properties coming to market before the listing is active. This is a great way to match up an agent's listing with another agents' buyer clients. At Summit Sotheby's International Realty, we have weekly update meetings about properties coming to market and new developments affecting real estate in the area. Agents from outside of our area will be oblivious to this information.

Check to see what kind of infrastructure and support staff the agent has available. If you're selling your home, your agent should be spending his or her time finding a buyer for your home, not personally designing flyers, writing and placing ads, and posting listings. I mentioned earlier the importance of professional and elegant photography, so you will want to determine if the agent uses a professional architectural photographer and videographer.

Things move very quickly in real estate and timely communication is a vital component of getting a transaction completed. When you're interviewing an agent or calling to set up a meeting, if it takes them two days to get back to you, that's not a good sign. Buyers may be in town for a limited time and if they want to see your home on short notice and your agent can't be reached, you may be wondering why there aren't more showings.

Agents work under a number of different philosophies and you should understand up front who you will be communicating with throughout the transaction. Some agents use a team concept and the work effort and communications is divided up based on what stage of the process you are in. It's better to understand the logistics in advance and know if the agent you are considering has systems in place for a seamless transaction. I work with an assistant and my agency provides significant support so I can focus on finding buyers for my sellers and homes for my buyers. I'm always the direct point of contact with clients.

## About Nancy Tallman

Nancy Tallman is affiliated with Summit Sotheby's International Realty in Park City, Utah, where she is one of the highest producing agents. She leverages her professional experience to provide innovative and effective marketing strategies, aggressive negotiating, and creative problem solving.

Nancy began her sales and negotiations career in California's health care field negotiating multi-million dollar contracts between physician groups, hospitals and insurance companies. Relocating to Park City in 2003 gave Nancy the chance to pursue her passion for real estate and her dream of owning her own business.

In addition to real estate, Nancy has been a leader of both professional and non-profit organizations. Nancy was President of the Park City Board of REALTORS® in 2015 and served as Dean of the Utah Association of REALTORS®' Leadership Academy in 2017. She is the 2015 recipient of the prestigious Utah Association of REALTORS® "President's Award," given to one of Utah's 20,000 REALTORS® each year, and the 2017 recipient of Park City Board of REALTORS®' "Meritorious Service" award. Nancy writes a weekly real estate blog at "insideparkcityrealestate.com", which is followed by thousands of readers throughout the United States.

Nancy perfectly balances a successful real estate career, raising two teenagers and two dogs, serving her community and daily activity. "I attend CrossFit classes or yoga at 5:15 am so they don't interfere with my other commitments. In the winter, I try to ski once a week and the rest of the year I take advantage of Park City's beautiful trails by hiking or mountain biking. One of my favorite aspects of being a REALTOR® is sharing the Park City lifestyle with others."

For more information about Nancy Tallman, visit www.InsideParkCityRealEstate.com

# Buying and Selling Luxury Homes on Maui

# Tom Tezak

## Introduction

Tom Tezak grew up in the Midwest and started his real estate career in Joliet, Illinois. After ten years of selling real estate in the Joliet area, he and his wife, Lori, decided to escape the cold winters and move their family to Maui with it's pristine beauty, rich culture, and unhurried pace of life.

Tom is co-owner/partner of Wailea Realty Corp., a boutique affiliate of Windermere Real Estate, with offices in Wailea and Kihei in South Maui. He specializes in helping clients buy and sell oceanfront and luxury properties island-wide. Tom also focuses in the South Maui resort areas, primarily in the communities of Wailea, Makena, and Kihei. He has been representing buyers and sellers on the island since 2000.

In this chapter Tom Tezak provides insights for buyers and sellers of luxury homes on the beautiful island of Maui.

## Selling Your Maui Home

With near perfect weather year-round, Maui is a resort destination throughout the year; however, we still have some home sales seasonality as consumers come to the island in greater numbers during the wintertime to escape the cold climate back home. This is the ideal time to have a home on the market, as most of our buyers are looking at homes while they are here on vacation. In fact, in a resort market, many people will visit while on vacation, fall in love with the lifestyle, and decide right then that they want to buy a property on the island. Our office is the most visible real estate agency within The Shops at Wailea in South Maui, and we have sold a number of our listings when people on vacation stopped into our office to see properties for sale.

Luxury properties are generally unique and here in Maui, because there are so many factors outside of the home itself that create value. It could be the amazing ocean views, location on the beach, privacy, proximity to the ocean, great shops, and restaurants, or a variety other factors. It's important to note that values can vary based on the consumer. For example, many consumers feel that the further a property is from the small business center of Wailea, the more values tend to decrease; however, there are other consumers, who value the distance, and solitude makes the value goes up. Privacy can be a factor for some, and a rocky oceanfront may be preferable to a sandy beachfront property, to avoid tourists or local residents having access to the beach in front of the home. Of course, the design, condition, and square footage of the home itself is also important, but it's a balancing act of trying to figure out how to price a property based on the house, location, amenities, and the area it's in. In addition, we also need to consider competing properties that may be on the market, as well as other similar properties that have recently sold.

When pricing a home, we need to make sure it's competitive compared to other properties on the market, so we are not priced out of the market and unlikely to attract attention. I believe that it is my duty to be a counselor to help the seller understand where the market is at, where it is going, and what to expect. If we're getting showings but not offers after the home is on the market, we engage with buyers' agents and the buyers after they've gone through the home to get their feedback. We assess whether it's the property or the price that is holding back offers, especially if they are buying a similar house. If it's the price, then we need to encourage our sellers to reconsider the pricing position and address it.

Presentation of the home to prospective buyers is critical both for in-person and online showings, so we need to have the home prepared to show before we take photos or start the marketing. For most of our owners, their Maui home is actually their second, third, or fourth home and they don't typically spend all of their time here. When they decide to sell their property, I prefer to meet them in person to discuss the process, but that's not always possible. Preparing and selling a vacation home comes with its own unique set of challenges, mainly because the owner is not likely to be on site, therefore a different level of responsibilities fall on the agent. If the owner is not present, it is important to have an agent who will effectively organize and communicate with all team members. When getting the home ready, as the agent, I will work as the "quarterback" with the owner's team to make sure that it is in show condition and looking its best. We will work with the property manager, cleaners, landscaping and pool service companies, and other contractors to get the home prepared and ready to show at any time during the listing period. Sometimes there's a better time of day to show the home, so we try to coach our buyer's agents into showing it at that time whenever possible.

The digital world has become so important to buyers, and as a result, we have to pay exceptional attention to detail in order to make our listings stand out. It is so important to understand that once the home is listed, there can be hundreds of showings of our properties, but we may never meet the buyers because they're sitting in their living rooms all over the world looking at them through the photos and videos. We need to showcase each individual home so that it will attract the attention of qualified buyers. Before exposing the home to the market it's critical to get all of the marketing materials, high- end professional photography, and videography in place before it hits the market, because those are the tools that are so important in today's world.

I feel that a broad-scope marketing program is ineffective when you're selling luxury property. The first step in crafting a marketing plan is to understand who a likely buyer for the home will be. Once this has been identified, we design a marketing program that will speak to that specific buyer. Is it going to be a family that's in their sixties or seventies with kids and grandkids? Or is this going to be a young entrepreneur that's looking for a bachelor pad or something that's going to be more unique?

In the Maui market, I have found the most powerful and compelling marketing tool to be a high quality lifestyle video. This isn't just a walking tour through the home; the video demonstrates the lifestyle that the home provides and it speaks to the specific type of buyer we think the home will attract. After previewing the home and identifying the likely buyer demographic, we write a storyboard and work with our videographer to develop our lifestyle video. Theoretically, when the targeted buyer is sitting there watching the video they actually put themselves in the home in place of the actor and think, "Well, that's my world."

The lifestyle video has become one of the most effective tools that I've used. Often agents doing videos want their videos to go viral and get watched 30,000 times. I've come to realize that I don't really care if 30,000 people watch my videos. What I find valuable is for one person to watch my video 30 times, because that's the buyer who keeps reliving the lifestyle when they go home. Once an interested consumer is here and looks at the property, they can take the online link with them, and in many cases, they will watch the video every day and continue to have the ability to experience living in that home. In a resort or vacation market it's critical for them to continue to be excited about the property and not get distracted with everything else going on in their world.

I learned the power of the lifestyle video from one of my listings. A couple visited one of my listings and a few weeks later we received an offer from their buyer's agent. The offer was rejected because it wasn't acceptable to the sellers. Another week later, we got another offer from that same agent and their buyers, and the sellers rejected it again because it still wasn't acceptable. Then finally, a little over a month later, we were able to come to terms with that buyer. After the sale was closed I was speaking to the buyer's agent and he indicated how important the video was in keeping the buyers engaged. Apparently, the wife watched the video every single day and she kept telling her husband, "I want this house." Had it not been for the video, they wouldn't have been so driven to get the house.

As we've said, this market has its own unique set of challenges. Just like our sellers aren't here all the time, our buyers aren't here all the time either. They may come in for a week or two on vacation and then be gone. As a result, we must try to accommodate showings when a buyer is here so that we can take advantage of every opportunity that exists. Sometimes, we only have a very short windows of opportunity to get that buyer in, so we need to try to do as best we can to make that happen.

One practice we sometimes observe in our market is the hidden, or "pocket" listing. There seems to be a mystique around a listing that's exclusive and not publicly available. I'm not a believer in this; I think that if you're going to put your house up for sale, it should be exposed. Not all agents are tuned into the hidden market, so ideal buyers might pick an agent that is not aware of such listings. So, for the most part sellers are really missing out on opportunities if they seek a pocket listing. There are agents that will promote the exclusivity concept, but from my perspective, in almost all cases that's not the best path for marketing properties. There are certain rare situations where possibly a high profile owner may not want their property on the MLS and I can appreciate that—but that should be very much the exception as opposed to the rule. At the end of the day, we're trying to generate as much revenue for the seller as we possibly can and get it sold in a timely fashion.

## What Sellers Are Saying

*"I have sold my two homes with Tom Tezak. He is quite knowledgeable and we got 100% of our asking price. Tom researched the market and helped set the exact right price. He then orchestrated the sale while I was on the mainland. He made sure all the details were taken care of and I had no effort in the sale but to sign the documents which were all done electronically until the closing. Even the closing was painless. I highly recommend Tom to be your Maui realtor."*

*"I honestly can't recommend Tom enough. Thorough, incredible, and an all around amazing real estate agent and guy! My favorite part about working with Tom is how open he keeps the communication and how easy he is to get ahold of. Highly recommend!"*

*"We asked Tom to interview with us because of having known the MacArthur family for some years. When we interviewed him, he came to our house extremely well prepared, with market comparisons, local real estate information, etc. After listening to Tom we realized that he is the expert and he was able to explain the opportunities which were ahead for us, primarily because of low inventory. He suggested a selling price range, explaining his logic in understandable terms and was able to reassure us with regard to our concerns if there were too many days on the market. Not long after we signed the listing with Tom, we returned to the mainland and Tom kept in constant contact with us if there were any concerns. Needless to say, we depended upon him a great deal and he came through with flying colors! We accepted an offer in just 8 days! Thanks, Tom."*

## Buying Your Maui Home

If you're considering purchasing on the island, it's important to understand your objectives and the lifestyle you desire before starting to look at specific properties. Although the Internet is a great resource to get information about the different areas of Maui, it doesn't necessarily answer some of the important questions that will help choose the ideal location for you. Even simple considerations such as traffic patterns or proximity to amenities are not easy to determine online. One of the first steps I take when working with potential buyers is to ask probing questions about their goals and plans. Some of these questions include, "Why are you buying? If it's a second home, it's not critical you buy before you leave the island. What are the reasons a home on Maui is attractive to you? How do you want to spend your vacation time? Is it because your love to surf and you want to be close to a surf spot? Is it because you're an avid golfer and you want to be part of a great golf community? Do you want a legacy to pass down to your children? Do you want to be able to walk to the resort and restaurants or are you seeking privacy while you are here?" It's import for the consumer to answer these questions honestly so that I can provide insight that will guide them to a location that will best work for them.

Oftentimes, potential buyers don't know exactly what they're looking for and having an engaging conversation with a good agent will help them to figure it out for themselves. Sometimes we meet with a couple that are buying, and one partner has one vision and the other partner has a different vision. Again, by sitting down in that conversation I can elicit the answers from both of them and very often we find out that they weren't on the same page. It's much better to have that conversation before visits to the properties, because if we go out randomly looking at luxury homes and we haven't had the conversation, one buyer may be going one direction while the other buyer is going the other, and we're not getting to the finish line.

If you want to be right in a dense tourist district, you might like an area like Kaanapali, Lahaina, or Kapalua on Maui's West Side. Alternatively, Wailea and Makena on the South Side also offer a resort district. South Maui is a bit less dense and more comfortable, but has a little less action as well. Surfers might want to be on the West Side because the surf breaks are better. Another thing to consider when spending time on the island is proximity to the airport and basic essentials like Home Depot, Costco, and other stores. Wailea is only 25 minutes away from the airport and business centers via two different routes, while the West Side resorts like Kaanapali are 45 minutes away, and there is only one road.

The first instinct is that a home right on the beach is preferable because you can walk right out into the sand; however, some buyers who may be more conscious of privacy, might want to be on a rock front because it's less likely that a tourist or local resident is going to be in front of their house. It's really a function of what the owner wants, the ultimate privacy or to walk out onto the beach. In this market we observe that high-profile, high-visibility luxury home buyers tend to migrate to the rock front because that gives them the privacy that they desire.

Maui has a good selection of condominium buildings and many buyers like the convenience that a condominium provides. It's not an uncommon path for some of our luxury condo owners to have a property here that they may decide to rent out on a daily basis to generate some revenue to help subsidize the ownership. This is common when the buyers are younger and they may have children, so they're less likely to visit as often. They may want to buy into the market when the prices are at a value point and own it for a few years renting it out while not on island. And then, as they get older and retire, they take it out of the rental program and keep it for a private space.

It's important to know that there is a distinction between residential and vacation rentable condominiums. Regulations restrict the rentals on residential condominiums to a minimum of six-month or longer terms, so there are not going to be tourists occupying the units. On the other hand, vacation rentable buildings allow the units to be rented out on a daily basis like a hotel room. It doesn't mean that you have to rent out the unit, but there is a lot of flexibility. When buying into a condominium it's important to know your goals before committing to one type or the other.

When it comes to negotiating the best deal for a luxury home buyer, I have some strategies that I like to use. One thing that I find works really well is a cash purchase offer and quick close. Most of the time, our luxury buyers are cash buyers that are liquidating investment funds for the purchase, which can happen rapidly. An all-cash offer with a close in 18 days often makes sellers sign things that they normally wouldn't sign. Very often a seller can't close in 18 days, but that kind of offer indicates a very serious buyer, ready, willing, and able to perform at a moment's notice. Such an offer has the power and impact on how flexible the seller is when it comes time to sign the contract.

I have another strategy that works really well if a buyer has an interest in multiple properties, but is motivated to make the best deal possible. If the buyer can fall in love with three separate properties, we can use our flexibility and latitude to leverage the emotion of one seller against the others in order to find what I consider "the real seller," and allow the buyer to get a great value. I will encourage my buyer to initially write two offers, one on the first choice and one on the second choice. I present the first offer to the seller's agent and say, "Here's an offer on your listing, but I want you to know that they also like two other homes an equal amount; this just happens to be on the top of their list. So, here's the offer—see if you can get it accepted." This motivates the seller to either accept the offer, or give us a more attractive counteroffer. If we get a counteroffer, then my recommendation to the buyer is to go and make an offer on the second property. We then tell the seller's agent, "I've got an offer out, but we got countered. Here's your opportunity for my buyer to buy your house instead of that one. If they'll sign this it's a done deal; we won't go the other direction." It's just leverage, and it vets out some of the sellers and provides more opportunity for the buyer to get the best deal possible on one of the houses they are interested in purchasing.

Most of our single-family luxury homes are not occupied on a full time basis, so year-round care of the property is important for the owners to have peace of mind. We have quite a few property managers that specialize in luxury properties. It's their job to check on the properties on a periodic (weekly, biweekly, monthly) schedule arranged with the owner. They are the key contact for the alarm company, so if there is ever an alarm, they are who is notified and they're reacting to it right away. The property managers are basically the owner's local eyes and ears checking to see if anything needs to be taken care of. There are some smaller luxury developments that have property managers that live right on site in a small house, and their entire job is to take care of the 10 or 12 houses in the development, managing the properties for the owners. Some homes also have caretaker quarters on-site, which is another great alternative. In that scenario, there's someone who lives on the grounds all the time. The property managers keep an eye out for things that need attention or repair and will notify the owner and coordinate the work with contractors. I also encourage my clients to contact me for a reliable second opinion if there is some major work that their property manager indicates is needed.

The other thing that owners come to expect from their property managers is that when they are preparing to spend some time at their home they're going to call their property manager in advance and request that everything be ready for their visit. This may include making sure the cars are fueled and washed, the home is cleaned, and the refrigerator and pantry are stocked with their grocery list.

One common misconception that I would like to address is that most of the land on the island of Maui is leasehold, meaning that you don't own the land. That's not true and most of the land on Maui is held fee-simple, which is the traditional manner of ownership in the United States. Fee simple means that you own that land and the structures on top of the land. Although there are a small percentage of properties on the island that are leasehold, it does need to be disclosed in the listing and in online descriptions of the listing.

## What Buyers Are Saying

*"We are very pleased again to have Tom's experience and counsel with the purchase of our second property about 10 years after the first. Our overall buying and closing experience with Tom and his team was very positive. Tom demonstrated a very strong grasp of the offerings' desirability, market conditions, and more importantly, he*

*presented the information in a rather objective manner. Just hours after our reconnect meeting in his office, we met him again to view, in an unhurried manner, the first set of candidate properties. Tom's judgment and opinion were credible. His comparative evaluations of the properties were fair and without any extra 'spin' or hype. He led the final negotiations skillfully. Twice, he was able to get the negotiations back on-track when they seemed to be going nowhere. He and his staff helped us buy our dream home. We have no hesitation in recommending him and his company."*

*"Tom is by far the best real estate agent we have ever had. He provides exceptional service and goes the extra mile for his clients. He has tremendous knowledge of the Wailea and Kihei markets. You can trust his advice and judgment. My wife and I had a wonderful, fun experience with him and would highly recommend him to anyone buying or selling real estate in South Maui."*

*"Tom is the best real estate agent I've ever had (total of about 7 transactions). He is there with you from beginning until end. We bid on two houses over two years and both became very complicated. He navigated very well and I knew I could trust him to represent our interests. In the end, we got a great house at a great price. There is no reason to even consider another agent."*

## Selecting an Agent

Whether you are buying or selling a luxury home, I would advise working with an agent that has solid experience helping clients with similar price range properties. Inexperience can be very expensive, so look for an agent that has longevity in the business and has knowledge of the local idiosyncrasies of the different locations within the market and how they affect home ownership and lifestyle. More often, an agent that has been involved in the market full time for five, ten, or fifteen years with a high volume of business should give the consumer some level of confidence. When it comes to a luxury transaction, a lot of money is involved, so it's really important to have an agent that this is not their first deal.

Look for an agent that wants to understand your goals. If you don't elaborate, and an agent doesn't ask many questions about your objectives in either buying or selling, it's going to be hard to get everyone on the same page and end up with a satisfactory result. My first step in talking with prospective clients is a counseling session where we get a good grasp on the goals of every person involved in the transaction.

One of the potential concerns that sellers have is giving someone else access to their property, along with security codes to enter the home. Creating a relationship, a good track record of performance in luxury home sales closed, and recommendations and positive reviews can help build that trust.

As the buyer is becoming an owner, relationships with property managers and service contractors are essential to make life on the island easy and comfortable. An experienced agent should have relationships with and be a good resource for a variety of resources such property managers, cleaning services, pool services, landscapers, handymen, general contractors, and others.

## About Tom Tezak

Tom Tezak graduated with a degree in advertising and marketing and was successful in early business ventures. He realized that his marketing background was a great fit for the real estate industry, and became a licensed agent in the Joliet, Illinois area. After ten years, he and his wife decided to move the family to Maui and re-establish his real estate practice on the island.

Tom has been representing buyers and sellers on Maui since 2000. He is co-owner and partner of Wailea Realty Corp., a boutique affiliate of Windermere Real Estate.

The agency has offices in Wailea and Kihei in South Maui. Tom helps buyers and sellers with their luxury and ocean-front property transaction all over the island and he also focuses in the South Maui resort areas and communities of Wailea, Makena, and Kihei.

Tom has received a number of prestigious awards and designations including:

- "Top 100 Realtors®" in Hawaii by Hawaii Business Magazine – 10 years
- Consistent Top Producer for every company he has worked for in the past 27 years
- Certified Luxury Property Specialist
- Certified Vacation Home Specialist
- Certified Negotiations Expert (CNE)
- Resort & Second Home Property Specialist (RSPS)
- New Project Specialist
- Tom is the host of Selling the Dream Podcast/Vlog on iTunes, Stitcher, Spotify, YouTube, SoundCloud, and more.
- Tom is the curator of 2ndHomeAgents.com, a community for resort and second home realtors around the world.

For more information about Tom Tezak, visit http://www.TomTezak.com.

# Buying and Selling Luxury Homes in Nashville

# Bruce Jones

## Introduction

Bruce Jones, a Nashville native, got his start in real estate at an early age. He was only 19 years old when his grandfather encouraged him to purchase a house to renovate and resell for a profit. He did this a few more times while in college and pursuing another career. Bruce decided to go to real estate school to get more education on real estate and earned his license. After getting his license, not intending to pursue real estate on a full time basis, he had a number of people ask him for help selling their homes.

A few years later, after gaining a great reputation in real estate, Bruce decided to pursue it full time and joined a small agency in the Nashville area. In 1999 he affiliated with RE/MAX and started building his team. Bruce helps buyers and sellers with their real estate transactions involving single-family homes, condos, raw land, new construction, and rental properties. He focuses in the Nashville area in Davidson and Williamson Counties, although he has represented buyers and sellers in over 20 counties in the region.

In this chapter Bruce provides insights for luxury home buyers and sellers in the greater Nashville area.

## Selling Your Luxury Home

When you're thinking of selling your home, it's best to clearly identify your goals so your real estate agent can help you achieve them. What is the reason for a sale and move? Is timing the sale a critical point? Getting the best price is always a priority, but is the home in a show-ready condition, or are there some improvements needed to present the property at its best? These alterations will most likely take some time and money. If improvements are needed, are funds available?

Although traditionally spring is a good time to bring a home to the market, the Nashville market is robust and people need to move here all during the year. I've sold houses here in every month and even every week of the year. The best time to list is simply when the house is in show condition and you're ready to move. There are more buyers looking for a home in the spring; however, there is also a lot more competition. The only time I would hesitate to bring a home to market would be during a harsh winter when bad weather is predicted for two or three weeks. We always want to build excitement and make a big splash when our listing goes live, so we wouldn't want to do that if prospective buyers may not be able to get out and visit homes.

A key concept for a successful sale is to price the home right and have it in show condition with a goal of selling it within 30 days of the listing. In my experience, the faster we can get a contract, the higher the probability of getting close to the list price.

Luxury homes are generally going to be unique and are likely to be custom homes that reflect particular tastes of the owner. The custom features and design, however, may not necessarily translate to value for all prospective buyers. Many sellers believe that their home is the best home on the market and should be priced at a higher than reasonable price. The critical factor is that a home has to be priced correctly or it's not going to attract much attention from buyers. Even in a strong market like we've enjoyed in the Nashville area, it's a mistake to overprice the home because there are rarely going to be any buyers who are willing to overpay by a significant amount. Also, remember that most home sales are going to be subject to an appraisal.

I will review similar homes that have recently sold as well as homes currently on the market to complete an analysis of market value. With real estate, location is always a big factor. Is the property in a preferred school district? Is it in good proximity for commuting to work for a good segment of buyers? Is there a view? Are there problems like road noise or other negative factors? These all need to be taken into account when assessing the home's value. I also encourage owners of luxury homes to review the competition on the market to get a realistic assessment of other properties that buyers are going to be seeing and comparing to their home. This can include viewing the competition online as well as driving by to take a look at some of them. Another tactic I'll occasionally use is to invite a few brokers I know to view the house and provide their opinion of the price, without letting them know in advance the results of my analysis.

Online sites like Zillow provide an estimate of price, but it's rarely correct. These online pricing estimators aren't meant to be a substitute for an analysis and evaluation of market value by an experienced agent or broker. They don't take into consideration the condition of the home, and there is no way they can evaluate the situation of the interior with respect to finishes, upgrades, or improvements. The algorithms used by these sites assume all homes in the immediate neighborhood are similar, and they generally use size as a differentiating factor.

Many homeowners update and improve their property to some extent over the course of ownership to increase the enjoyment of their home. Improvements probably increase the value of a home, but as a seller, you should understand that it's unlikely that the increase in home value will be more than the cost incurred. This is particularly true if renovations were made a few years ago and now appear dated. Trends and buyer preferences change over time. A kitchen remodel that's several years old may not reflect what buyers currently are looking for, and they may view it as needing an update. Replacing old heating and air conditioning systems, appliances, or a roof are part of home ownership, and buyers expect all of these things to be functional, so replacing something that is not working isn't going to increase a home's value.

Everyone likes new construction because it's crisp, clean, and has a new smell. The walls are freshly painted and the kitchen sparkles. That's why new homes typically sell at a higher price per square foot. When selling a home, it's important to strive toward making the home fresh, clean, updated, and crisp. It may not be new, but it needs to be like new.

A buyer's first physical impression when walking up to a house is critical. Landscaping needs to be free of weeds, with shrubs trimmed and the lawn cut. Homeowners typically don't use their front door often, so it's easy to overlook. But that's where buyers enter a home, so make sure your front door is as clean and fresh as possible. Wooden doors can be faded from the sun, so a fresh coat of paint or stain will make it inviting. And be sure to clear away cobwebs around the front door or porch. Although it's important to repair rotted or deteriorating windows or wood trim, windows on the front porch should receive particular attention to make sure there isn't any chipped paint. While an agent showing the home is getting the key from the key box and preparing to unlock the door, there are several seconds when the buyers will be surveying the outside of the entrance and forming opinions about its appearance even before walking through the house. People tend to remember their first and last impressions and forget some of the things in between, and most likely buyers will remember their first view just before entering.

A home's interior needs to look as fresh as possible. Carpeting needs to be cleaned and walls should be painted if the paint is chipped or if there are dark or bright colors that would not be enjoyed by the typical buyer. Kitchens are a key deciding factor for most buyers. If it's very dated, the home is going to be a tough sale. Trends change frequently, and an update a few years ago may not be current now when you are ready to sell. If you're going to do some updating, you don't have to invest in the most expensive materials. As an example, I wouldn't recommend picking an exotic cut of granite that costs $300 per square foot that you think looks great when you can get something that looks good for $50 per square foot.

There are some circumstances in which it may not be practical to complete a fix-up before placing the home on the market. An example might be when there is extensive hardwood flooring that has a dated stain color or needs to be refinished. Let's say the owner isn't able to move all the furniture out, have the work done, and then move everything back in again. We will get pricing on redoing the floors from reputable contractors and have that ready to present to buyers who are concerned that the work will be very expensive. I have a good list of reliable, established contractors that I've used over the years who I know will do a great job, and they are reasonable in cost as well.

Odors are one of the things that make any home difficult to sell. When I'm working with a seller, I'll have a very blunt conversation if unpleasant odors are present. If I can smell the odors, buyers looking at the house will smell them as well. These are most often caused by pets or smoke, and you really have to remove the cause of the smell, not just replace it with cover-ups like scented candles. Typically, the carpet will need to be replaced, and maybe the walls will need to be painted as well.

Families accumulate a lot of possessions over time, and their homes tend to start filling up with furniture, pictures, and many personal items. We want to be able to present the home to buyers in a condition that's as neutral as possible so they can imagine living there. And that's difficult to do when the seller's home is crowded with furniture and their own personal effects. It can also be distracting for buyers as they are more likely to look at all of the stuff and not focus on the rooms. Another consideration is that rooms look smaller if they are full, and buyers walking through may be afraid their furniture won't fit. I'll advise sellers on decluttering the home by removing some furniture and personal items if rooms appear too crowded. These things can be packed away before we start showing the house.

If you have pets, you'll need to have them away from the home during showings or at least have them crated. I love dogs, and most dogs are very nice and wouldn't hurt anyone, but there is a portion of the population who are afraid of dogs.

Online exposure is key for all listings today and most of the time is what makes the first impression. If a listing doesn't show well online, it's going to limit the amount of interest in a showing. Great photos are critical in creating a good initial impression and opinion on the property. It's important to make sure the home is show-ready before the photos are taken. We always want to use a professional photographer who knows how to take pictures from the best angles and in the best lighting to really showcase the home. If the property has a view or is adjacent to open space, aerial drone shots or videos will really show off the view. Walk-through videos of larger homes are very effective as well. I'm also doing 3-D schematics of floor plans. Once the home is ready to show and we have the photos and videos ready, we can start exposing the home.

There are some important concepts for maximizing the initial impact as the home listing goes live. Online viewing is very visual, and most people looking for a home are going to be getting alerts when new listings appear, or they will be looking for new listings periodically. What we don't want to happen is for the listing to go live before the photos are loaded. Buyers who see a listing without photos are just going to swipe past that listing and are not likely to return. We want to have all of the photos and videos completed in advance and loaded at the same time as the data on the property so we can have a complete listing immediately. Also, we have our listings made in the morning so that we maximize the amount of time that first day that the listing is considered a "new listing." If the listing goes live in the afternoon or evening, the number of hours that it shows up as a new listing is severely limited, and many buyers may miss it if they're primarily focusing on new listings.

The Nashville area attracts a significant number of buyers relocating from other parts of the country, and with the vast majority of buyers initially searching online, wide online exposure is critical to reach potential buyers. My listings are syndicated to a large number of online platforms, and I have also found that exposure through social media, like Facebook and Instagram, is also important. Glossy magazines that feature luxury homes are another good way to expose the home to potential buyers. They are distributed in auto dealerships and other places frequented by affluent people. These print advertisement magazines generally have an online version as well, so the featured homes will be exposed to buyers regardless of their location.

When marketing a luxury home, the lifestyle of the location needs to be marketed as well as the home. If the home is in a golf community, show pictures of the golf course and club. If it's in a walkable neighborhood with proximity to amenities, feature some pictures of the shopping, restaurants, and other amenities. If there's a community fitness center and pool, add pictures of those facilities.

After a contract is signed, lenders who are financing the buyer's purchase will be scheduling an appraisal to substantiate collateral of the loan. Although we generally don't experience an issue of an appraisal coming in lower than the selling price, I make a detailed list of improvements and "behind the wall" features that may not be obvious. I work with the sellers to identify all of the improvements and features with dates completed along with the cost and give the list to the appraiser. This provides additional information to the appraiser and may help justify a higher market price, especially if the home is highly improved.

In summary, selling your luxury home for the highest price depends on a number of factors, including establishing an appropriate list price, getting the home in very good condition, making necessary preparations so it will show at its best, presenting it professionally, and exposing it widely to buyers.

## What Sellers Are Saying

*"We would absolutely give Bruce Jones the highest recommendation possible. He made our entire selling process extremely easy and stress free. First, he has so many contacts and is so knowledgeable about the area. He started networking for potential buyers before we even had our home formally listed and we had a contract within the first week. Next, he handled the negotiating and inspection phase with very minimal stress on our part (and most of it was late at night and on the weekend). He is completely on top of every detail and just does not let anything slip through the cracks. Finally, the closing details were a breeze thanks to his great staff that handled everything except our signatures. To top it off, he even found an interim home for us to rent while our new home is being constructed. Without a doubt, I would never use any other realtor in the Franklin area."*
　- Cindy M.

*"Bruce and his staff are just outstanding!! I don't generally like writing reviews but I felt compelled because of 1) above and beyond service 2) it was because of reviews on this website that we chose his company. We live in California and wanted to sell our home in Tennessee once our tenant moved out. Bruce and his staff handled everything: promptly, professionally and personally. Being out of state could have made the process of selling a home so much more stressful. Having the right team made this not only so much easier but actually enjoyable. We felt so relaxed and knew that everything was being handled. From helping us getting the house ready to sell, talking price and strategy, and everything in between, this could not have been a smoother process. The house was on the market for less than 2 days when the house was sold! Thank you again Bruce."*
　- April E.

"Bruce and is staff are excellent at what they do. He has assisted me in selling multiple properties, and his service is always excellent. Thorough, knowledgeable, and very communicative throughout the process. I'd highly recommend Bruce to anyone looking to buy or sell a home in the middle Tennessee area."
    - Larry M.

## Buying Your Luxury Home

One of the first steps when planning to purchase a home is to define priorities when choosing a location. School quality is generally going to be one of the priorities for families with children. Proximity to work and traffic patterns are important, as well as access to the airport for people who travel frequently for their business. What kind of lifestyle is important to you? Some people prefer to be in a walkable community with shopping, restaurants, and other nearby amenities. Others may want more space and prefer a more rural property. I've observed that many young professionals may work in the suburbs, but prefer to live downtown where there are more entertainment venues. We have a wide range of luxury properties in the greater Nashville area that can fit just about any lifestyle.

I encourage buyers to think in terms of resale when they're choosing a location. Although you may plan to live in the new home for a long time, life happens, and circumstances may dictate the need for a move a lot earlier than anticipated. It's best to avoid a situation in which you knew upfront the home you're purchasing is going to be hard to sell at a later date. One example of this is a school zone's reputation. Even if you don't have children and schools aren't a priority for you, the school zone can play a part in the future marketability of the home. Two nearly identical homes on either side of a county line can have a significant difference in value, and the one in the preferred school zone will be easier to sell in the future.

As you are listing your priorities and deciding on the locations that best fit what you are looking for, you should be preparing to organize how you will be funding the home purchase. Most luxury home buyers have a pretty good idea of what they can afford, whether it's going to be a cash purchase or if they will be using mortgage financing. Sellers and sellers' agents are typically not going to consider any offers or usually won't even show a home unless the buyer provides some proof of funds or pre-approval. If a mortgage will be used, a letter is required from a lender indicating that the buyer has been pre-approved up to a certain amount. It's also a good idea for buyers to clearly understand the amount of the loan they are qualified for as well as interest rates and monthly payments.

Once the priorities and a budget for a house are established, it's time to start looking at homes. As I am showing buyers around the area and helping them define priorities, we are getting a good idea of locations that will work for them. The buyers are usually looking at online listings, and I will be developing a list of appropriate houses to look at as well.

Some people believe that they will enjoy a higher level of appreciation if they are one of the first buyers in a new custom home development. This can happen, but there is risk regarding the quality of homes as the development is being built out. I've seen some new large developments that started out with nice custom homes, but later the developer sold some of the land to companies building lower cost houses. Even if there is a so-called estate section, appraisers and agents will be looking at comps in the neighborhood as a whole, so it's possible that appreciation could be limited in the future.

The real estate market has been strong in Nashville for the past several years. There's a diversified economy, and many companies are expanding or relocating to the area. With continued population growth, the inventory of homes has reduced, so it's been more of a seller's market. Homes that are priced correctly and are in great condition are selling rapidly and sometimes are receiving multiple offers. Once you identify a home you want, you need to be prepared to move rapidly or risk having another buyer make an offer on the home.

There's a lot of variability on how well sellers have prepared their homes for sale, and it's not unusual for buyers to visit homes that meet most of their criteria, yet cosmetic issues hold them back. If a house has the right location, a great design and layout, but maybe the paint colors or the seller's furniture is a big drawback, then this could be a great opportunity, and it probably will translate into a lower sale price. Consider that even if you are buying new construction, there are likely to be some cosmetic improvements you'll be making anyway, such as painting some of the rooms. Try to envision what a room would look like in a lighter color if it's too dark for your taste. We can get trusted contractors in to suggest ideas and price out the cosmetic improvements while we are in the due diligence period, and the work can be completed in a short time period right after the closing before you move in. The end result could be just what you were looking for at a lower price.

When you've found the house you want, it's time to consider making an offer. I will provide an objective analysis of market value, but at the end of the day, it depends on what price the buyer is comfortable with. I like to have a discussion with the listing agent prior to making an offer to find out the seller's motivation for selling. Frequently we can find out what is important to them. For example, it could be timing a move before the start of a school year. Not many agents do this, so we can have an advantage in structuring an offer that is more likely to be accepted.

Some people think that negotiations should start with a "low ball" offer. With a strong market, this is not likely to be a viable strategy and can backfire. It can be taken as an insult, be rejected without any counter, and the buyer may be viewed as someone who cannot be taken seriously. It's just not the way to open up a conversation with the seller, and in a competitive market, the seller is much more likely to work with someone else who brings in a reasonable offer. There are exceptions to this, such as in the case of a distressed situation in which the house has been on the market for a long time or when a corporation owns it and there are no seller emotions involved.

I have observed buyers finding a pretty ideal home, but the price negotiations are moving toward say $5,000 or $10,000 more than they wanted to pay. Is it going to be a big disappointment if they don't get the house? If so, they should look at the extra monthly cost of the mortgage, which is not going to be very much.

An experienced agent will guide a buyer through the process of negotiating a contract, getting the inspections and other due diligence completed in a timely manner, and assisting the buyer all the way through the process to the closing.

## What Buyers Are Saying

*"Bruce has helped us numerous times in locating properties perfect for our needs. He is the best at real estate. Has a nack for understanding even the small things and stays active all the way to closing. He has saved us money and made us very happy. HIGHLY RECOMMEND."*
    - Paula D.

*"Bruce is excellent in his field. He has represented for the sale of a home and the purchase of two homes. He has a wealth of knowledge regarding the market and has an extensive amount of resources useful to anyone purchasing or selling a home."*
  - Joanna E.

*"Bruce was referred to us by a very reputable realtor in Florida, where we were relocating from to the Nashville area. He knew more about Nashville and the surrounding cities than we ever imagined! Not only did he exceed our expectations in regards to house hunting, but he educated us on all aspects of home buying and relocation, in general. His professionalism and hospitality relieved all of the stress that accompanies buying a home. Though we ultimately decided to push back our move date, we won't even think about contacting anyone other than Bruce to assist us with our future home search in Nashville, TN. Exceptional individual and an expert in the field."*
  - Nikki

## How to Select an Agent

Whether you are buying or selling, a real estate transaction is a major event, and you should have an experienced and knowledgeable agent assisting you through the process all the way to closing. It takes a team of people to complete a sale or purchase, so look at your agent as the team leader at the center of the hub. A leader should be confident in his or her ability and have a good grasp on market data. Experience is generally obtained over a number of years, and I would suggest working with an agent who has successfully been through the process hundreds of times. If you are selling, the agent should be asking enough questions to make sure your objectives are clear and that the agent can help you realize your goals.

If you are a buyer, and especially if you're new to the area, you will want to make sure to choose an agent who is familiar with all the locations, developments, and neighborhoods that may be of interest to you. Ask questions to see if the agent's answers seem credible. For example, ask questions like: What trends have you seen over the years? If you have children of school age, where would you live? Where's the best value for my money right now?

You will be working closely with your agent over a concentrated period of time. Make sure you choose an agent you feel confident will work with you to look out for your best interests and help you achieve your goals.

## About Bruce Jones

Bruce Jones is the team leader of the Exceptional Living Group, associated with RE/MAX in Brentwood, Tennesse in the Nashville area. He is a seasoned broker with over 20 years of experience in real estate and has been ranked in the top 2% nationwide. Bruce has completed hundreds of transactions working with buyers and sellers since 1996.

Bruce helps buyers and sellers with their real estate transactions for single-family houses, condos, raw land, new construction, and investment properties. He has personal experience as an investor and as a venture capitalist, building and financing new homes and new construction developments. He is involved in ongoing new construction projects in Davidson and Williamson Counties that are not listed until near completion.

Bruce is a Certified Luxury Home Marketing Specialist (CLHMS) and also has ther following designations: ABR, CRS, GRI. Tennessee Real Estate Broker License # 260577.

For more information about Bruce Jones, visit http://www.FranklinElite.com.

# Buying and Selling Luxury Homes in the Dallas Area

# Mark Cain

## Introduction

Mark Cain has been interested in real estate and construction since an early age. While he was in school, Mark's mother worked for a real estate company and he enjoyed going with her to look at new developments that were going up. He also took classes in high school that were related to architecture and buildings.

While attending the University of North Texas, Mark started working at a market research company, and continued to work for the company after college. It was an unintended career; however, he continued receiving promotions and after several years worked his way up to senior director.

After several years in market research, Mark decided to jump into real estate, where his true passion was. After earning his license, he found rapid success with a new construction luxury listing in Preston Hollow. From that point he began building his real estate career using his background in market research and advertising. In his first year he became a top producer in his office and in his third year he made the cover of a local quarterly real estate magazine in Dallas.

Mark has been affiliated with Dave Perry-Miller since 2004 and is a consistent top producer at the firm as well as in the Top 1% of all agents in the Dallas/Fort Worth metroplex. He typically works with sellers of luxury properties in the Preston Hollow and Park Cities area of Dallas.

In this chapter, Mark provides insights for buyers and sellers of luxury homes in the Dallas area.

## Selling Your Luxury Home

First and foremost, the market is always price driven. The most important thing that you can do when you want to sell your home is price a property knowledgeably and appropriately for the current market conditions. It doesn't matter if there is a stunning marketing campaign. The home will not sell at an unrealistic price. That will only generate lowball offers and the home will languish on the market. It's critical that the property be priced competitively and compellingly from the very beginning.

The most obvious value that a real estate agent can bring to a seller is the knowledge and experience to accurately price a property. There are many factors that go into valuing a property like location, condition, and market comps for similar properties in a similar location. Estate properties are so unique that placing a value on a property is more of an art than a science. It takes someone that's been in the business a long time, who has been inside many sold properties as well as current competitive properties, that will have the best knowledge of where a particular property is likely to be valued.

If the market is active, I'll review sales that best match the client's property over the past six months as well as similar active listings and homes under contract. If the market is slower, or as we move up in price point, I'll look at comparable sales over the past year or longer so we can get some historical perspective on where the likely value will be.

There is a selling cycle in the luxury market in Dallas. The majority of home sales typically occur in the first half of the year. We usually see enormous buying activity in the first and second quarters. The summertime market in Dallas is extremely slow because of the heat and temperature index here. People of means who might be in the market for luxury homes are typically spending time in cooler climates during the hot summer months. The market tends to pick back up in September and until mid-December. If you are looking to sell a luxury home, the best time to put your home on the market is in January, March, or September to hit the strongest market activity.

At higher price points there are fewer buyers, so luxury properties tend to stay on the market for longer periods of time than lower priced properties. It's important to consider that there's not a lot of urgency in buying activity at the upper price range.

Presentation of the home to the market is critical. Most homes that fall into the luxury category are fairly well maintained. Even though this is true, every home needs to be de-cluttered, cleaned, repaired, and presented in its absolute best possible condition to the market. Every other home on the market is competing with your home and you want to win the beauty contest. This means making it as appealing as possible. The Dallas market prefers everything to be new so you want to make the home look as much as possible like a new or updated home.

It takes a trained eye to know how well a home is going to present itself to potential buyers and it's not always obvious to the homeowner. One of the benefits I provide to my luxury home clients is a staging and preparation evaluation by a professional staging company here in Dallas. They will walk room-by-room and make a detailed report about editing, de-cluttering, and recommended minor changes or replacements, like paint color changes or repairs that need to be made in order to freshen the home and make it photo-ready and showing-ready. The seller can use the report as a guide to getting the home prepared for sale or can choose to hire the staging company to execute the changes. This is a great option for busy executives or professionals or when the seller has multiple homes and is not in the local area to organize the work.

After the home is prepared and is show-ready, it's time to capture the elegance with high-quality photography. Studies show that 97 percent or more of homebuyers go to the Internet as their first source of information for a home, so it's critical that the house is presented beautifully and professionally online. A professional real estate photographer, who has the experience of presenting multi-million dollar homes, can capture the beauty of the home with bright and inviting tones. It's important to capture the key features and elements with the right angles as well as the best lighting. In addition to still photography, there is interior videography, aerial drone photography, a custom website for the property, and two videos—one, about three or four minutes in length to use on the property website, and a short video, about 30 seconds long, to use on several social media platforms.

Once the home has been prepared and the photography is completed, the property can be widely marketed to get maximum exposure among qualified buyers no matter where they are in the world. The home will be put into the multiple listing service (MLS), which provides exposure to over 12,000 local agents. I always develop a color brochure with the complete property description and color photographs. A floor plan can also be made. There will be an office tour of the property so the other luxury agents within our company have the opportunity to see the house in person, and I'll also host an open house for cooperating luxury agents and brokers in the area. Although luxury homes on the market may not always have a "For Sale" sign in front, I recommend it for my clients. My firm is the market leader in Preston Hollow and the Park Cities so our sign carries a lot of weight. It's a luxury boutique brand name that buyers in the area perceive means that the home has been appropriately prepared for the market and knowledgeably priced. As a result, we tend to not have offers that would come in that would be unattractive or not negotiable.

In our digital age, direct mail is an often-overlooked effective source of advertising. Using direct mail we will inform homeowners in nearby luxury neighborhoods of the new listing. Neighbors in and around the area of the property can often be one of the best sources of advertising! They may have a friend, a colleague, or know someone who is looking in that area. Very often, neighbors can become a virtual sales force that helps direct a buyer to the property. In addition to sending out direct marketing to neighbors in the area, we'll also send out a special mailing to the top 300 agents in the area. This is a good way to get the listing some exposure in the market and reaches real estate agents that were not able to come to the open house. Another tool that I have developed over time is a weekly e-mail blast that is called "Mark Cain's Friday Update." This report goes to about 10,000 agents in the area every Friday, and it provides a status update of all my listings. For example it shows listings under contract, open houses scheduled, price changes, or any other status update that agents might need to know in order to pass that information along to their clients.

As previously mentioned, the vast majority of homebuyers are going online to start searching for a home, so wide online presence is key. Complete data on our listings is posted to hundreds of real estate Internet sites locally, nationally, and internationally. It's important to specifically get the listing on luxury home sites that are focused on homes over a million dollars. Executives relocating to the Dallas area are an important source of buyers, so we also reach out to the global market with our affiliation and contact with relocating companies to the area.

When it comes time to show the home to potential buyers, it is extremely important that the agent or representative be present at the showing. This is so important because they can show the property in a way that allows the viewers to really understand all of the unique components of the property. The listing agent has an understanding of the price point, the geography of the property, and even the personality of the property. This provides the best chance of getting the homebuyers to connect with the property and even see themselves living there. If the buyer's agent is not familiar with that property or that part of town, we have the ability to then give a tour of the house and provide all of the details. We can also provide information about schools, restaurants, shopping, distance to airports, etc. so that buyers can be familiar with the property, the area, and the lifestyle that the property would afford them. We will plan on arriving at the home at least 20 minutes before the showing. While waiting for the those who will be viewing the home, we'll turn on all of the lights, have music playing in the background, turn on waterfall or pool fountains (if applicable), and even adjust the thermostat when needed. This process ensures that the home is ready to be viewed and the buyer's agent can focus completely on the clients and the property. For all of our million plus listings, I always co-list with another handpicked agent that I feel best fits the situation. In this manner one of us, or our administrative assistant who is also a licensed agent, will always be available to be present at a showing on short notice.

Selling luxury homes means that we are dealing with high net worth individuals such as professional athletes, business executives, professionals, authors, and musicians. For the most part these clients don't want their private business to be made public, so maintaining privacy is of utmost importance in serving them. We have a policy within our company and within our group that we will not divulge outside of our group, or our company, the identity of buyers or sellers that we are working with to the extent that we can within the limits of public records. In the Dallas area property tax records are public so anyone can pull up a listing from the Internet and determine who the owner is. Shielding the owner's identity can be avoided by putting the property ownership in the name of a trust or the name of the company. At the time of purchasing, buyers can do the same thing to limit knowledge of the ownership. There can be tax disadvantages to doing this, so we encourage our clients to seek the guidance of their real estate attorney and/or CPA.

## Buying Your Luxury Home

Most people that purchase luxury homes tend to do so with all cash. Some will purchase with mortgage financing for tax reasons or to gain higher returns on investments when mortgage rates are low. As a buyer you should expect to be able to show evidence of your financial capability. Evidence can be in different forms, but usually will be statements from banks or other financial institutions or from a financial advisor. If planning on mortgage financing it will be in the form of a lender's pre-approval.

Time is our most valuable and equal commodity, regardless of one's standing in life. When we take on a buyer client we want to make sure the client has the financial ability to purchase a home in the price range they have declared interest in. We don't want to waste the time of our client, any homeowner, the buyers' agent, or our own time by working with an unqualified buyer. It is simply unfair to everyone involved. We will request written evidence of financial capability and will also verify it with the client's financial institutions or advisors. What I have found is that high net worth people usually have no problem providing this information so long as it is kept confidential and private. They don't want to waste anyone's time and they don't want their time wasted either. The majority of owners of high value properties may also require some proof of a buyer's ability to afford their home before a showing. They may have priceless works of art and other valuables in their home and want to verify that someone is qualified to purchase before going inside of their home.

Most buyers moving within the Dallas area will have a good idea of a neighborhood where they want to live, but someone moving into the area can benefit from help in matching their objectives with available locations. As a buyer it's important to be as thorough as possible in identifying your needs and wants so your agent can best assist you in finding your ideal home. We start the conversation either in person or on the phone getting a sense of the work location and what is important for your lifestyle and household needs. Typical considerations include budget, type of property desired (single family home with a big yard or high rise condo), type of area (urban/uptown or suburban), school needs, commute to workplace (drive or rail), importance of access to airport, and proximity to amenities (golf club, shopping, restaurants, and entertainment). The more clarity we have on these factors the better we can identify the best locations that will work for the client. From that point we can lead a tour of different parts of Dallas that best match and so that they can see the styles and vintage of homes that are in different neighborhoods.

After a home is chosen, we'll help the buyer make a knowledgeable offer. Just like an analysis we would perform when working with a seller, we'll study and present comps for the most similar homes that have sold in the price band and general area over the past six months to a year. We'll also look at similar properties that are currently active on the market. Due to the uniqueness of multi-million dollar properties, estimating market value is an art that is developed with time and experience.

I've found it particularly useful to talk with the seller's agent to try to determine the seller's motivation for the sale. Although the agent may not always be forthcoming, many times they will provide some insight on how negotiable the seller is on the price as well as other terms or points that may be of major importance to the seller. With as much information as we can glean from the comps and the seller's motivation, we are better prepared to help the buyer make an appropriate offer.

Keep in mind that although you are buying a home that is a financial asset, it's an emotional transaction for all parties involved. From the seller's standpoint, it's not just their asset; it's a place that they have lived in, and where they have celebrated birthdays, anniversaries, and other life events. Therefore, it is necessary as buyers to treat the negotiation with the utmost of respect to the seller so they are not offended. It is also important to note that the sellers may still also be members of the community and just relocating to another residence here, so they will want to see the buyer as someone who will become a member of that community. You don't want to have a bad reputation in the community because you were unfriendly in the purchasing process. At the end of the day, it is a financial transaction but it needs to feel like a win-win situation for both sides and it needs to be done with dignity and respect.

The purchase contract will allow for a time to complete inspections on the property and you will want to have a complete objective report on the health and condition of the house before closing the purchase. The inspections will assess the condition of the home and all of the equipment. If the inspection report indicates issues of concern, that can lead to additional negotiations relating to repairs. One of the benefits of working with a seasoned, experienced agent in the luxury market is that that agent will have a list of trusted and respected vendors for inspections and services. A list of recommended vendors not only is a benefit during the inspection process, but after the closing you will have a good resource for companies that can make changes and repairs, and also maintain the property and associated equipment.

Here in Texas, title companies are a critical part of transaction process and selection of the right title company for a multi-million dollar transaction is important. I always recommend choosing a title company that has attorneys on staff at the location because there are occasionally title issues or survey issues that arise. Because the price point is so high, every square inch of the property has value. If there's a lien or encumbrance on the property that was unknown prior to the title work being pulled and delivered then there needs to be a quick and easy resolution of that issue. Involvement of an attorney is important to provide a legal perspective and a resolution that will be binding on the buyer and seller.

## How to Select an Agent

When you are buying or selling a home, there will be a close relationship with an agent, so it's important to feel comfortable and trust that the agent representing you is going to be looking out for your best interests. The agent is not the decision maker, but is going to be there to provide guidance and counsel so you can make the best, most informed decisions throughout the process. It's an emotional transaction for everyone involved and you want to be satisfied with the end result. A luxury home is a major financial asset, so when choosing an agent look for experience with successful completed transactions representing buyers and sellers of homes in a similar price range and location.

In representing a seller, I'm selling the whole property, every room in the house and every square inch of the yard, so it's important to review and know everything about the property, so the complete story can be conveyed to prospective buyers through phone calls, in person, or through advertising in various media outlets. Although many agents work independently, there is an enormous benefit to working with an agent that has a team. Most potential buyers have limited time and expect to see a home on limited notice. Being always available for showings is critical to getting a home sold, and having a team approach assures that there will be an uninterrupted around the clock coverage for the home. Life happens, and an agent is going to have medical or dental appointments, an occasional vacation, or a child's sports event or activity to attend. With a team, duties for attending showings or answering questions can be shared to make sure someone is always available.

When representing a buyer, I want to make sure that you love the neighborhood, the part of town, and the specific home that you choose. Where you live and your surroundings are critical to how your life works and can either make your life function optimally or can inhibit or encumber your life. As an agent I take my responsibility very seriously to make sure we find a property that meets as much of the criteria communicated as possible, while keeping the budget and financial objectives in mind. I want to make sure that if you decide to sell in a few years down the road that I can be the listing agent for the sale and make you whole on the way out.

## What Clients Are Saying

"Mark sold my last home in under a week and found us our new home. I am so happy with his service. He really knows how to market and uses the best photographers. He is very knowledgeable in the Preston Hollow area."
  -user 51468692

"Mark Cain is a fantastic professional realtor. When it came time to sell our own home and move to Las Vegas, Mark Cain was our choice and he got the job done. Mark is simply a 'Class Act' and handles himself in a very, very professional manner."
  -Becky Z.

## About Mark Cain

Mark Cain, a Dallas-area resident for more than 30 years, is familiar with many of the most sought-after areas of North Dallas, Preston Hollow, Park Cities, and Uptown. Soon after earning his real estate license, he became and continues to be a top-producing agent. He has been affiliated with Dave Perry-Miller since 2004. Mark has earned the "Fine Homes Specialist" designation and represents many high-profile properties in the Dallas area.

He has consistently been voted as one of *D Magazine's* "Best Real Estate Agents" since 2003.

For more information about Mark Cain, visit http://www.MarkCainProperties.com.

# Buying and Selling Luxury Homes in Northern New Jersey

# Joshua Baris

## Introduction

Joshua Baris entered the real estate industry in 2002, initially representing commercial property owners, but fairly soon went over to the residential side. After a few years he took a corporate job selling home warranties to all the major real estate companies in New Jersey and turned his territory into the most profitable in the Northeast. The national economy was at a low point in 2010, but Joshua wanted to get back to his true passion – selling residential properties. Despite the general economic lull, he became successful right away as he reentered the industry. He was Rookie of the Year for his first year, despite only selling during a few months of the year. He has since significantly grown his business every year. Joshua has continuously ranked in the Top 1% of Licensed New Jersey Real Estate Agents. Real Trends and "The Wall Street Journal" recently named him for the third consecutive year as one of "THE

THOUSAND," the Top 1000 Real Estate Professionals in the United States.

Joshua focuses on the luxury residential market in Bergen County, adjacent to New York City, although he also helps sellers and buyers with their transactions in other adjacent counties. In this chapter he provides his insights for luxury property buyers and sellers in Bergen County and the Northern New Jersey suburbs.

## Selling Your Luxury Home

Luxury home owners generally have a number in mind when they are considering selling their property. One of the most important things to understand is that there's always a market value for each individual property; however, it's not necessarily the value the owner feels it's worth. When considering selling your home, you should expect your agent or potential agent to provide a detailed comparative market analysis for your property with comparables reflecting recent sales in the area, if there are any. At higher price points, the skills of the agent are extremely important because there are going to be fewer similar recent sales, so there's a lot less data to use. The agent should be able to confidently support the analysis with facts that demonstrate the rationale for the estimated market value. It's okay to have a debate with an agent on the market value, but if the analysis is based on objective facts, it's going to be difficult to dismiss.

One trap for sellers, especially those with expensive properties, is the evidence that there are a lot of agents who will just take a listing based on what the seller states the property is worth without any discussion or analysis. There's a big risk of wasting a lot of time and finally realizing the price expectation is not at all realistic, and maybe you wouldn't even be considering selling if you knew the real value. Some agents will take a listing just on the hope of making a sale, even at much less than the client is expecting, because even on a substantially reduced sales price, the agent can earn a large commission. It's better to know upfront the realistic value and not be disappointed later. I'd suggest being very skeptical of an agent who just agrees with your idea of a price and doesn't bring in any independent research to substantiate the number.

I work with a multitude of builders that specialize in high-end residence speculative new construction. As a general rule, most builders are listing a home for sale while it's still under construction. I'm a strong advocate, however, for waiting until a new house is fully finished, including painting and cleaning, and then staging it before trying to market it for sale. For many of my sellers, this advice has continuously proven to result in higher prices and a faster sale. I have a history of taking over listings that have not sold with previous brokers/agents and selling them in only a few months' time, while the previous agents were unsuccessful for years beforehand.

Buyers have a hard time envisioning themselves living in a vacant house, and they have a hard time imagining how their furniture and other possessions will be placed. There's little to see that matches to their lifestyle. Although many people think a vacant room may look larger, studies have shown that an empty room appears to be smaller, and as a result, potential buyers may even believe their furniture won't fit.

I suggest to completely finish the construction of the new house and then stage it with furniture, decorations, and accessories so potential buyers can fully appreciate the property and imagine living there. This includes staging the bedrooms, bathrooms, kitchen, and living areas. Bedroom staging should include linens, and bathrooms need the right soaps and towels. Sofas and other furniture should be staged in the living rooms along with other furnishings that match the right motif of the home. A bar would be stocked with fine liquors, and if there's a wine cellar, it would be stocked with some fine wines. The whole concept is to make the home look and feel extremely inviting. I've accumulated a large inventory of furniture and furnishings that can be used in my listings to completely stage empty luxury homes at an appropriate level for the property.

I also edit and stage the furniture in occupied homes. This may include adding or removing furniture and accessories to make the house look its best for marketability purposes.

When a home is properly staged and show-ready, it's time to capture all of the elegance in professional photos and a video. It's critical to use a photographer and videographer who specialize in real estate. I don't want a photographer who focuses on shooting models all day. Instead, I want someone who knows which angles of a home look best and how to make a room shine in all its glory. It's similar to choosing a physician — if I needed to have brain surgery, I wouldn't trust an orthopedic surgeon to provide me with the best possible outcome and deliver the proper results.

In our area, we're not just targeting local buyers. Many potential buyers are in New York, busy working all day, or they may even be living overseas. We want to give viewers a very good glimpse of what a particular property has to offer and why it will be attractive to them without even having to see the home in person. Each individual home will likely be attractive to certain lifestyles, so it's important to make sure the home appeals to the most appropriate buyer lifestyles when creating the photos and videos. We try to include all the key elements that our targeted buyer is looking for.

Here's an example of a recent listing that demonstrates how we would tailor the video to match with an expected buyer. In this particular example, the home is elegant with a very open floor plan and not so much a family-oriented estate. I believe there are two different types of buyers who will be most attracted to the property. The first is a bachelor, or someone else that's young, who is looking to entertain in the home. The other is a Chinese buyer. The home has a lot of lion faces throughout, and that's very powerful and masculine in the Chinese culture. There's also a lot of red used in the home as well as elements of feng shui. Our video shows some aspects that are going to be attractive to a Chinese buyer, such as the lion heads, the right colors, lakes and streams with moving water, sunlight, and the openness of the home. As we are looking to attract bachelors, we made sure to show the bar area, the sitting area at the pool, the steam room, the billiards table, and other amenities of that nature.

Depending on the expectations of a buyer for a property, we will use fine luxury automobiles in the videos. They could be a Rolls Royce, Lamborghini, McLaren, Porsche, or something similar. Particularly when we are trying to attract international buyers, the proximity to Manhattan is crucial. The potential international buyer may have no idea where our cities in New Jersey are located, but they want the luxury and access to New York. We want to demonstrate that the property may only be a 15 to 30 minute drive after seeing a show in Manhattan with their family. So, we'll film a ride in a luxury vehicle from Manhattan, across the George Washington Bridge, and to the home in real time so they can feel the elegance as well as the proximity.

I utilize a full video production and editing crew for my listings. We typically spend anywhere from 12 to 30 hours filming a luxury property, making sure that every single selling point of the property is captured. We'll spend up to 100 hours editing. All of my videos are shot in 4K high definition.

I'm a firm believer in leveraging technology in the real estate field to get an advantage for clients selling their home. By this I don't mean just posting the listings on the typical websites that most brokers and agents use. We've got the high-quality video, now it's time to strategically place it so targeted buyers can see the property, get excited about it, and have a desire to learn more. I create unique websites for each of my listings to showcase the video along with all of the other information about the listed property. The web domain could be something like SaddleRiverLuxuryEstate.com, for example. Then I drive buyers to the listing website to view the video. Unlike the typical way it's done in the industry, I don't post the video to the common real estate websites. What I want to do is capture the buyer's interest on my unique listing website and have everything they need to know right there.

When someone is watching a video on YouTube, for instance, at the end of the video, the viewer is just presented with different videos to watch, and they are more likely to get distracted and not return to my listing video. When we post our listings on the common real estate websites, we will provide a link to the video on my listing website, and once there, viewers can find everything they need to know about the property. Another reason I do this is to build authority of the listing website using search engine optimization (SEO), because a key factor for a website coming up in online searches is the amount of traffic going to the website. If I've now got thousands, or in many instances tens of thousands, of visitors to the website to view the video, now the search ranking for the website is going to increase dramatically. In this example, when someone is interested in buying a luxury home in Saddle River and they search online for a specific city, words, or even phrases, they're more likely to be presented with my listing website near the top of the search results. Social media sites like Facebook, Twitter, and Instagram are also important places to feature the property, also with links back to the video on the listing website.

Another way I use technology is to target specific groups of buyers that are a good match for the listing. I have a very large database of potential buyers classified by demographics, needs, geography, and lifestyle. The database includes contact information, including email addresses and mobile phone numbers. When I'm marketing a listing, I use my buyer database to reach out to a targeted group of people who are most likely to appreciate the property. For example, if the property would appeal to families with children, one group I might target is buyers with families in Manhattan who may be interested in moving to the suburbs. If the property is likely to be attractive to Asian buyers, I'll send the information to my buyer list in China, Japan, Korea, and possibly other countries.

I'm not afraid to try new technology-related initiatives to market my listings, and I try to stay ahead as an innovator in this field instead of being a follower. So, I will experiment with new ideas and expand those that prove to be working. For example, a new project I'm implementing is placement of mobile phone charging station kiosks in one of the area's largest hospitals. Each of the kiosks includes a TV that plays my listing videos. These stations are set up in the physician's lounge, an outpatient waiting room, reception area, and public cafeteria. Physicians are one demographic that are potential buyers of luxury homes, and based on the location of the hospital, there are many affluent patients and family members who may be at the hospital. Since they may need to charge their phone, that's another way to expose listings.

As the marketing efforts attract prospective buyers, it's important to make sure they are really qualified to purchase the home, even before a showing. There are a number of reasons for this. First, showings can be an inconvenience for the owners if the property is occupied because they may need to tidy up the home and be away during the showing. Second, people with expensive homes don't want just anybody walking through their house. There are privacy concerns, especially if the owner is a celebrity or public figure, and most likely the owners' valuables will be in the home. Before showing one of my listings, I always require buyers, or their agents, to provide proof of funds or a pre-qualification letter from a financial institution if mortgage funding will be used to purchase the property. Proof of funds can take many forms. It may be a letter from the buyer's CPA or financial advisor, or it may be a financial statement prepared by an accountant. Experienced agents advising buyers seeking a luxury property understand the need to show proof of funds or pre-approval, so this normally will be arranged in advance as a normal course of business for qualified buyers. One exception I would make on this policy is if the buyer is generally known to be a high net worth individual, such as a celebrity or professional athlete.

We also want to avoid getting into a contract with a buyer and unfortunately finding out after the fact that the buyer does not have the financial means to close on the property. Now we have taken the property off the market for a period of time and diminished it's marketability to actual qualified buyers. Buyers may think they can afford a certain price, but they might not have considered that they already have substantial debt on other properties or fine automobiles and are not able to leverage as much as they thought for an additional property. This is another reason to maintain a policy of only showing the listing to pre-qualified buyers.

Negotiations are always going to play a big role in getting the best price for the property. Luxury property owners as well as buyers for these properties are successful people who are where they are today by being good negotiators and by always expecting to get the best deal. It's not uncommon to have a large gap between initial offers and the listing price on several million-dollar properties. Although the principals may be good negotiators themselves, it's better to let the agents handle the negotiation communications because a home sale or purchase is an emotional transaction, and it's easy for a buyer or seller to say something that will insult the other party that might kill the possibility of a deal. When choosing an agent to sell your home, make sure to pick one who has the right negotiating skills and tools to properly represent your interests in reaching the best possible deal.

## What Sellers Are Saying

*"After trying unsuccessfully for several years to sell our home, we brought Joshua on board as the listing agent. We devised a new strategy and in just over one week received three offers! Josh did an excellent job in using these offers to negotiate the best possible price. In addition to his professionalism and knowledge, he was a pleasure to work with, always available to answer any questions and stayed involved throughout the process. We highly recommend him."*
   - Karen and Louis R.

*"When we decided to sell our home, we knew that finding the right real estate agent was crucial to our success. After interviewing several agents, we decided to go with Joshua Baris because of his confidence and exceptional knowledge of the housing market. Our decision proved to be the right choice.*

*"From the very beginning, Joshua showed personal interest in us as the sellers and was always available to discuss any questions or concerns we had throughout the process. In addition, his superior marketing skills helped our home stand out amongst a large volume of homes for sale in the area. As a result, we sold our home for the price we wanted and within a short period of time.*

*"We would definitely recommend his service to anyone seeking a real estate agent. You will not be disappointed by making the same choice that we made."*
 - Sam and Maria D.

*"I knew Joshua Baris back in elementary school, but I had not met the successful man on the billboards I would see all over town. I followed him on Facebook and looked at his website every so often and what I really enjoyed was the constant new listings (that showed me many sellers trusted him) but more importantly was the constant SOLD postings (usually right below where it was just listed as a new property). So when it came time to hire someone to sell my family's home I knew Josh would be the right choice. My dealings from our first meeting to close can be summed up in 4 WOW's:*

*"1- Upon first meeting Josh we said "WOW" this guy knows not only from a sales perspective the history, area, comps, and competition but presented a marketing plan that truly shows you why he is the most innovative broker in the marketplace. From the arsenal of contacts he has to the technology in knowing how your property will be perceived and marketed will make you feel confident you will have a buyer.*

"2- After signing with Josh we said "WOW" that was quick. Within 24hrs of listing our property with beautiful pictures and video taken I was texted with many showing appointments from his team that is truly at the top of their game. We had our first offer in 48hrs of listing.

"3- "WOW" Josh really works hard. Whether a 6am showings or a 9pm it really doesn't matter he will be there and will answer your calls/texts at any time of the day.

"4- "WOW" he's actually a good guy. Our property sale had some bumps in the road and Josh was persistent in taking into account our timetable and always worked in our best interest.

"All in all I was very happy with the job Josh and his team did for me. He did exactly what I expected him to do, and he made me look good to my family for knowing he was the right guy. Thank you once again Josh, and your team!!"
   - Ben W.

## Buying Your Luxury Home

The first step in preparing to purchase a home is to make sure you know how you'll be funding the purchase. It may be all cash, or you may need to secure mortgage financing. Many people with the ability to pay cash may decide to secure mortgage financing, particularly when the interest rates are low. They may believe their money can earn a higher return invested elsewhere. As I mentioned earlier, a seller's agent is generally not going to even allow their client's home to be shown unless the buyer can demonstrate proof of funds or pre-approval of a mortgage that will allow for the home purchase at the listing price. Getting prepared in advance will minimize the initial frustrations when you want to start looking at homes. The other point is to know in advance the price of a home you can afford. Let's say you believe that $1.5 million is approximately the price of home you want to purchase. You might even consider homes listed up to about $1.7 million to take negotiations into account. If you start looking online for homes in this range before even knowing for sure what you can afford, you will be disappointed and may have wasted a lot of time if you find out later that you can only afford about $1 million.

So, if you're going to use mortgage financing, get that lined up first. Most experienced agents have some lenders they can refer. I have a number of mortgage brokers and lenders that I know can expeditiously provide a pre-approval and guide my clients all through the financing process.

Organizing your objectives as a buyer will help you and your agent focus on locations and properties most suitable for you. Many of our buyers are moving to the suburbs from Manhattan. They work in the city, but maybe they want to raise their family in the suburbs. Transportation and ease of commuting will likely be an important aspect of a home search. Depending on the mode of transportation, commuting to work, and whether their office is in Midtown or the Wall Street area can make a big difference when choosing a location. School system rating is also a critical factor. If the buyer's children have special needs, proximity to an appropriate school will be a consideration. We have a wide range of cultures represented in Northern New Jersey, with an amazing variety of schools that cater to individual cultures and languages, so that could be a factor when selecting a home. Lifestyle comes into play as well when deciding on a location. Proximity to fine restaurants, shopping, entertainment, and other amenities is important to some buyers.

It's not always obvious what locations will best match a buyer's many objectives. That's where an agent with comprehensive knowledge of the broader suburban area, even across multiple counties, can truly be a resource to find a location that works best. Many agents are focused on a very small area, maybe even just one city, so they may not be able to help someone who needs a broader overview to find the best location. I've strived to become educated on the entire suburban Northern New Jersey area so I can be the ultimate resource when it comes to helping buyers find the ideal location for their specific requirements. I've compiled a comprehensive list of resources for buyers on my main website, www.NJLux.com, that has information on transportation, school ratings, and amenities by city or area. I've also sold homes in over 50 cities throughout the area.

After choosing the best general location, it's time to start looking at specific properties. Most buyers will do some of this online, and their agent will generally come up with a list of candidate properties to visit. After visiting a number of homes, hopefully you will find one or more that you are interested in pursuing and are ready to move toward an offer. But how do you know that the listing price is right? The buyer's agent should be able to provide an educated assessment of fair market value. This is done with a comparable market analysis that looks at all aspects of the property and makes a comparison with the most similar recent sales, adjusting for differences among the properties being compared. The agent should be able to provide details that rationalize the fair market value estimate. It's not unusual to find that the list price is higher than the analysis shows, so that's where the agent should be able to advise on an offer that leaves room for negotiations to get the property for the best price. The negotiation process may take multiple counter-offers to finally come to an agreement on price and terms that both parties can accept.

The process isn't over when a contract is negotiated and signed. The buyer has a due diligence period to make sure the home and mechanical equipment are in good condition. Your agent should have a list of qualified home inspectors that can rapidly complete inspections and provide advice if there are issues. Sometimes specialists from specific trades should be brought in to assess the situation if issues are found with mechanical, electrical, or other systems. The agent should be navigating you through the entire process as you move toward the closing.

## What Buyers Are Saying

*"Josh, Thank you for all you have done- your expertise, guidance, friendship and humor made buying a house a wonderful experience! Not an easy feat. You kept us laughing when we were nervous and guided us when we needed real advice. We found an amazing house thanks to your professionalism and knowledge of the market. Thanks again Josh, we will miss our nightly text chain!"*
　- Sari and Mike

*"Josh was very helpful though our entire home buying process. He took the time to show us many houses and would walk us through the positives and negatives of each. In addition, he would provide creative ideas about improvements that could be made, which helped us develop an opinion. Most importantly he would say no when he thought a house was not a good deal. Throughout our time with him we never felt that he was driven by the commission. Instead he was looking for the right result for us."*
　- Michael R.

*"Josh is different from most Tenafly, NJ Realtors, in that he's an agent who truly makes you feel as though you've got a friend in your corner. He's very honest and will never steer you wrong, as he strives to understand your needs and find the perfect home to match. Josh is the most honest realtor I've ever worked with, and I've worked with quite a few prior to meeting him. He's passionate, driven, and*

*determined to find you your ideal home. He cares, takes time to listen, and by the end will be not just your agent but also your friend."*
  - Tali S.

## How to Select the Best Agent for You

Whether you are buying or selling a luxury home, you should expect to have an expert on your side who will look out for your best interests and guide you all the way through the process. A multimillion-dollar home is a huge asset, and selection of an agent or broker to represent you is one of the most important decisions that will determine success in meeting your objectives. Be sure to look for an agent with a strong track record helping luxury property buyers and sellers with successful transactions closings. Great reviews and testimonials can be indicators of success. Volume of individual transactions is another indicator.

If you're selling your property, you should expect that your home will be properly presented, exposed, and marketed to potential buyers in the demographics that represent likely buyers. Ask the potential agent how and where the property will be marketed. Make sure the agent is consistently investing in marketing their listings in a variety of ways to maximize exposure. There's generally a correlation between how agents market themselves and how well they market their listings. If you're looking for a top luxury agent, do an online search for luxury agents in your area and see who shows up in the search results. As an example you could search for "Saddle River luxury home specialist." Follow the links to the agent websites showing up in the results and see how they are presenting and marketing themselves. Do they have an interesting and informative website that represents them as a high-level luxury property specialist, or do they just have a generic page on their agency website? You can gain a lot of knowledge about an agent's marketing just with this simple exercise. Look at their listings. Do they use high-quality photography and professional videos to get potential buyers excited? When interviewing an agent, find out how they reach ideal buyers for luxury homes. Do they just put the listing up on the typical real estate listing websites, or do they have a way to target very specific buyers that could be interested in your home — in the local area, in Manhattan, around the United States, and internationally?

As a buyer, being able to gain insight on communities encompassing multiple counties will help you find a location that is best for you and the long-term enjoyment of your home and the community. Particularly if you're moving to the suburbs from Manhattan or from another area, you're going to want to work with an agent with wide area knowledge who can guide you to a location that's going to be the best fit for you.

## About Joshua Baris

Joshua Baris is the Founder and Owner of NJLux. He uses a variety of innovative technologies, strategic on-line marketing, key word optimization, and social media to excel in selling New Jersey luxury properties.

Joshua has continuously ranked in the Top 1% of Licensed New Jersey Real Estate Agents and he was recently named for the third consecutive year as one of "THE THOUSAND" by Real Trends and "The Wall Street

Journal" as one of the Top 1000 Real Estate Professionals in the United States. "New Jersey Monthly Magazine" named him a FIVE STAR® Real Estate Agent in 2017, for a 7th consecutive year. He has also been featured as the Cover Agent of "Top Agent Magazine" for 4 consecutive years. He was the #1 luxury residential real estate agent in 2016 in Bergen County for listings sold over $5,000,000. In the spring of 2017, Joshua joined the new Global Luxury Division of Coldwell Banker Residential Brokerage.

He is an active member of RELO, and works with a number of relocation companies. Joshua has relationships with many executive and senior level management within Human Resource Departments for major Fortune 5000 companies in the area. He assists their employees with relocation and housing needs.

Joshua has been referred to as the "Celebrity Realtor to the Stars" as he appeared with his clients Coco and Ice T on the E! Networks hit reality show "Ice Loves Coco," helping them to obtain Coco's world headquarters in Weehawken, NJ. He regularly works with other celebrity and professional athlete clients.

He is frequently interviewed in the news media for his New Jersey real estate knowledge. Joshua and his listings have also been featured on primetime TV including "Living Large" on CBS and "Open House NYC" on NBC.

Joshua focuses his New Jersey luxury real estate practice by selling luxury estates and luxury condos throughout Northern New Jersey cities including, but not limited to Alpine, Tenafly, Cresskill, Demarest, Closter, Norwood, Old Tappan, Harrington Park, Haworth, Mahwah, Ramsey, Upper Saddle River, Saddle River, Montvale, Montville, Woodcliff Lake, Hillsdale, Westwood, Ho-Ho-Kus, Kinnelon, Wayne, North Bergen, West New York, Weehawken, Secaucus, Hoboken, Jersey City, Totowa, Oradell, River Edge, Rutherford, Englewood, Englewood Cliffs, Fort Lee, Cliffside Park, Edgewater, Wyckoff, Franklin Lakes, Ridgewood, Leonia, Teaneck, Rockleigh.

For more information about Joshua Baris, visit http://www.NJLux.com.

# Buying and Selling Luxury Homes in the Suburban Boston Area

# Elena Price

## Introduction

Elena Price entered the real estate profession shortly after graduating from college and has been working as a real estate broker for more than 25 years. Although she has been licensed in three states, Massachusetts, Georgia and Rhode Island, Elena's primary business is now concentrated in the suburban Boston market, and she specializes in the towns of Westwood, Dover, Needham, Dedham, and Walpole. Elena is currently affiliated with Coldwell Banker Residential Brokerage with an office in Westwood, Massachusetts.

In this chapter, Elena provides insights for buyers and sellers of luxury homes in the suburban Boston area.

## Selling Your Luxury Home

My experience is that owners of luxury homes in this area are typically very savvy in business and they have a good understanding of the market and what other homes are selling for in their respective areas. As a broker, I always believe that it is an excellent idea for any seller to get an independent opinion from an experienced agent that can identify comparable sales and likely has personally viewed many of the recent sales and competition that is currently on the market. Overall trends in the market should also be considered and understood so that opportunities are not being missed. After reflecting on their personal views, comparable sales information, and trends, it is always the sellers that make the final decision on price. These decisions, alone, can often dictate if a house will sell, or not, and how long the sales process may take.

For the local market as a whole, the busy seasons are in the springtime and then in the fall, with minimal activity in the winter. There's also a different dynamic at the higher end of the price spectrum. Purchase activity for luxury properties can be driven by many different factors including, but certainly not limited to, relocation activity, job promotions, private school acceptance notices, salary increases, and year-end bonuses. Sales are made throughout the year, but the highest level of sales activity for luxury properties is between October and February and, typically, this sector of the real estate market also picks up again mid-March, immediately after private school acceptance notices are received.

Critically, when luxury homes go the market, the home needs to be ready to show to potential buyers, which means that it has to look perfect. Most of the time luxury homes are extremely well furnished, as well as maintained inside and outside. Professionals have generally designed the interiors and exteriors. But occasionally there are situations where some preparation is required to get the home ready to present to buyers. If the home hasn't been redecorated in a long time, we will encourage the owners to make some improvements to make the home look aesthetically pleasing. This might include painting, re-carpeting, and hardwood floor re-finishing. It also may include replacing bathroom and kitchen counters and appliances. I also often encourage sellers to have their own home inspection before the house goes to market and to repair and/or take care of any items that are identified by the home inspector. This allows the seller to be more aggressive in pricing since the home that is going to market is truly "move-in-ready."

Often, however, homes may just be so personalized with photos, artwork, and personal items that it's too crowded and less than ideal from a marketing perspective. In this case, I often suggest that the homeowner hire a professional stager to come in to de-personalize and de-clutter the home. When buyers are viewing the home, we want them to be looking at the attributes of the home itself, not all of the personal belongings, especially if they create a distraction. Buyers need to see themselves in a new home when viewing it, not the sellers.

If the owners have moved and the home is empty, we will also recommend staging the home with furniture and accessories. An empty home doesn't show well and buyers have a difficult time imagining how their furniture will fit in an empty room.

Most people searching for a home are going to be viewing online before ever viewing homes in person. Therefore it's important that a home is listed on a variety of online real estate platforms. Buyers for homes in this area are often located in other states and often times, even from other countries. Our listings need to attract attention, because any seller probably only has a few seconds to make a first impression where the viewer wants to learn more. The wording used to describe the home needs to include all of the features that buyers will find appealing. Otherwise, a seller and their broker may never hear from them.

Perhaps most importantly to selling any home is that everything needs to look perfect, so professional photography and videos that capture the beauty of the home are critical when we are presenting the home to online viewers. The home needs to be in "show condition" and staged when we do the photography. I will frequently even hire two different professional photographers to get different views and perspectives so I can choose the photos that best show off a home. I will also use aerial shots to show off the surroundings and the view. Videos can also be impactful, especially when we narrate the video, describing the features of the home. I will also have exterior shots done in advance in different seasons if the home is not ready to go on the market. Yards look beautiful in the spring when everything's in bloom and the fall colors are beautiful as well.

Further, immediately before any listing goes on the market, I like to invite my company's network of luxury agents as well as those from other companies in the surrounding area to an open house to view the property. In this way they can become educated about the home and we can answer any questions they may have. Once the home goes on the multiple listing service, they will have already seen it and can speak intelligently about what the home offers.

As we move up in price range, the pool of potential buyers diminishes in size, so it's important to know the trends for buyers of expensive suburban properties and how to reach them. Often, luxury buyers are coming out from the city and are looking for land and more space to raise their family. Many foreign buyers are investing in fine properties in this area as well. With all of the colleges around Boston, international buyers will often buy a luxurious home for their family to use while their children are in college. This may be for visits while their children are attending college and it may also provide a place for a vacation or a retirement home later. The Boston area is also a major high tech and biotech hub, with many growing companies in the area. New hires, including executive are moving into the area to work at these companies. Additionally, we are seeing some major corporate headquarters relocations to the area. One of the more prominent recent announcements was the relocation of the GE headquarters to Boston.

In marketing any luxury home, I always utilize as many channels as possible in marketing a luxury home, but oftentimes it's proactive networking that's going to get a home sold. Thus it's important for your broker or agent to know and have relationships with other luxury agents as well as people who can afford to purchase these types of homes. Within my company, there's a certain designation that allows an agent to sell high-end luxury properties and we are all connected and in constant contact. In our local market there is also a lot of networking among top producing brokers that focus on luxury properties, so that opens up additional avenues to market the listing.

Other important ways to expose the home to buyers include social media and print advertising, especially where the readership includes executives and high net worth individuals. For example, I will frequently advertise listings in the Wall Street Journal, Boston Magazine, and other publications targeting the demographics of potential buyers.

As we are attracting interested buyers, it's important that before showing the property we know that the potential buyers are qualified to purchase the home. There are several reasons for this important step. First, most luxury home owners are extremely private. They may be corporate executives, high-earning professionals, professional athletes, and other public figures, so they want their privacy protected. Second, they probably have valuables in the home, and don't want people casually in the home where they have many things of value. Third, it's an inconvenience for the owner to show their home, as they may need to tidy up and leave the home during the showing. Put simply, it can be an enormous waste of time for all involved if the people viewing the home are not really qualified. In fact, without these pre-qualifications it is certainly possible that by the time a potential purchaser and the seller have realized that a potential purchaser can't afford a particular home, the home would have been taken off of the market for a period of time, all of which should never occur when the buyer is not qualified in the first place.

Many buyers of luxury homes also often purchase with cash, so some documentation proving available funds should be obtained. This might be a proof of funds letter from an accountant or financial advisor, a letter from an attorney, or a bank statement. If the buyer will be using a mortgage for part of the purchase price, a pre-approval letter from a reputable lender should always be required. If the buyer is working with an experienced agent, the agent will know that this type of documentation is necessary and will provide it upfront. Potential buyers are generally receptive and understanding of this procedure and it gives the seller a sense of confidence and helps to demonstrate the earnest intent of the buyer.

Although every situation is different I always try to make sure to know enough about a potential purchaser when they are ready to make an offer so that both my seller client and I are comfortable moving forward to a successful closing. It also helps if I know or have a familiarity working with the buyer's agent. If that's not the case, it's important to remain very diligent protecting the seller's interest throughout the entire process. Making sure the parameters are set right up front and the buyer knows our position on relevant terms, minimizes the chances for misunderstandings that would lead to further negotiations later in the process.

## What Sellers Are Saying

*"It is with great pleasure and appreciation that I share comments on my experience with Elena Price in both the selling of our home and the purchasing of our new one. I encountered a broker with a high level of knowledge and experience.*

*"From the very beginning, Elena guided us through the process. After several unsuccessful attempts to sell our home, working with Elena proved to be the right choice. She assisted us in every step of the way in getting our home prepared for selling and we had an accepted offer at the first open house.*

*"Elena also was instrumental in facilitating the negotiation and purchase of our dream home. She is truly dedicated, hardworking and her knowledge of the market and process is invaluable. She always*

preserved the perfect balance of professionalism, lightheartedness, patience and diplomacy. Elena is a true delight to work with and is by far the best - a true professional in a class all her own. Thank you for a job well done!"
   - Dianna J.

"I would highly recommend working with Elena Price. Her knowledge of the local area and the process of selling and buying a home is impressive. She is easy to work with – patient, calm and straightforward. We worked with Elena in both selling our home and purchasing another and we were grateful to have her guidance and advice. Elena's dedication to her clients was incredible and she is highly accessible. She made the whole process so much easier than I had anticipated! I am so glad that we chose her as our agent."
   - Jane G.

"Elena was right on top of every aspect of selling my home and made me feel that she was almost as invested in selling the home as I was. She is honest, direct, knowledgeable, yet compassionate! Thank you!!"
   - Suzanne M.

"We were extremely pleased with Elena's performance as our realtor throughout our listing and selling process. She assisted us in the sale of our Westwood home, and made the process so smooth, easy and stress free. Elena is a consummate professional with an incredible knowledge and expertise. She is also a wonderful, caring person, a delight to work with."
   - Pat & Tom O.

## Buying Your Luxury Home

Most people planning on purchasing a home start looking online to get an idea of homes that are available in their area of interest. When you know that you are going to be making a move, it's best to engage an agent to help you decide on an area and to find the best home for you. Massachusetts is a buyer agency state, so it's in the buyer's best interest to hire an agent that they can trust to help them with the transaction. Any agent representing a property only represents the seller as their client. By having a buyer's agent, you will have someone looking out for your best interests.

Although most listings can be found in the multiple listing service and online today, there are many properties that may be available that are not listed. As an example, I often have listings or know of homes that are not listed that might be a good fit for a particular type of buyer. Sometimes this happens when a property is not ready to come to market. There are other times when the seller wants to keep information about selling their property private. By working with an experienced agent in the area, you may be able to have access to properties that may not be showing up online.

Clearly identifying your needs upfront will help when selecting a location to live. Commuting time to work is a factor for most people, so access to public transportation and highway routes will be an important consideration.

Rail service may be desirable for some people. Some of our towns offer close access to Amtrak Northeast Corridor and Acela Express Train service to New York and other cities.

Families with children will be concerned about school ratings. They may also be interested in locations near one of our private schools, which we are known for in this area, just outside of Boston. Demographics of the towns will also be a consideration before deciding on a location. Each town also has it's own particular tax base and the services provided to residents are closely related to the tax structure.

An agent with good experience in the suburban area will be able to assist in understanding the individual characteristics of the various towns and be able to help find a location that is right for you.

Before actually viewing homes in person, I recommend that you identify how you will be paying for a property. Sellers and their agents want to make sure that potential buyers viewing their home have the ability to afford it. If the purchase will be made using cash, then it's customary to provide a proof of funds letter that displays the buyer's ability to afford the property. The letter might be from an accountant or financial advisor that has detailed knowledge of the buyer's financial situation. Even if the there is the ability to pay cash, a mortgage may be preferred for part of the purchase price, sometimes for tax purposes. If seeking mortgage financing to close the purchase, the buyer should arrange pre-approval from a lending institution or broker in advance. The lender or broker will typically provide a pre-approval letter that will indicate that the borrower is already approved for a loan up to a certain figure. Having either proof of funds or a pre-approval in advance provides a level of confidence to the seller that the potential purchaser has the ability to close on the home purchase.

After deciding on the location and viewing homes, most buyers typically will have a few candidate properties that they are considering. At this point, local knowledge and market expertise can help narrow down the selection process. Buyers at the higher price point tend be very educated about overall market value and price per square foot. They're able to understand value by the quality and details in the home. I will assist by going over the pros and cons of the homes being considered and provide information on pricing that similar homes have sold for in the area. Perhaps most importantly, my first-hand knowledge of the different aspects of comparable properties can be used when a buyer is ready to make an offer on a particular property.

It should be noted, however, that when a property sits on the market for a long time buyers typically are thinking that the home is either overpriced or that there is something wrong with it. They may think that there's an opportunity for a great deal by offering well below the listing price. Although this occasionally can be the case, the reality is that in the higher price range, our market for qualified buyers is much smaller than for an average sale priced homes. And while we do have a large amount of luxury properties available, we have fewer purchasers looking to buy those homes. The other thing that every buyer must consider is that at higher price points, the sellers generally do not have to sell. Purchases at this level are discretionary, but so are the sales, so generally there's no sense of urgency and the sellers can hold on to the property until they get what they believe it's worth.

Before making an offer I always like to talk with the seller's agent as well to get an understanding of the seller's priorities. Sometimes there are certain aspects other than just the price that will influence the negotiations. For example, the seller may be interested in timing of the close or having the flexibility in the timing to move out. Often the home's furnishings will come into play as well. By knowing the seller's goals in advance we can be better prepared to submit an offer that will attract the seller's attention.

Equally important, something to consider when purchasing a home is privacy while you own the home and even when you may be selling it some time in the future. One strategy is to take title in the name of a Realty Trust or an LLC. In this manner, your name is often not immediately shown in the public real estate records.

The real estate purchase and sale transaction process varies somewhat from state-to-state. In Massachusetts we have a two-step process. In the first step we have an offer document that includes the key terms like the price, date, list of any contingencies that need to be removed, and a small deposit. Typically all of the contingencies, except for financing, must be removed before proceeding to the second step. This would include having inspections performed with the results being satisfactory to the buyer.

Time can go by quickly so we want to order inspections immediately after the offer is accepted. The inspections typically include the structure, roof, mechanical and electrical systems, and others, depending on the property. I have a list of recommended inspectors that have a good history of quality work for my clients.

The second step that usually follows 10 to 14 days after the signed offer is a formal purchase and sale agreement that is drafted by attorneys for the buyer as well as the seller. When the purchase and sale agreement is signed a more substantial deposit will be collected that will be the seller's recourse, if in fact, the buyer did not enter the contract in good faith. If the seller does not perform as according to the contract, the deposit is often refunded to the buyer. The closing usually occurs about a month after the purchase and sale agreement is executed.

## What Buyers Are Saying

*"We worked with Elena on looking for a home in the Westwood, Norwood, West Roxbury, Dedham area. Elena was a pleasure to work with! As first time home buyers she guided us through everything with a professional and positive manner. She provided us great advice throughout the home buying process and we eventually found our dream home with the help of Elena."*
- Aislinn S.

*"We loved working with Elena! She sold our house and helped us purchase a new home."*
- Heather B.

## How to Select an Agent

There's no substitute for experience when it comes to selecting an agent to represent you in a luxury home sale or purchase. One of the things to look for is years of experience in your particular community as well as in selling luxury properties. Certification as a luxury property specialist is one indicator to look for whenever working with a real estate broker. Having a strong company behind the agent is another important point. Good knowledge of the marketplace and keeping current with trends are also always important. Make sure that the agent has a good knowledge of comparable properties in the area from being involved as an agent in transactions of similar properties as well as being able to visit comparable properties when they have been on the market.

If you're looking for someone to sell your home, make sure the agent has a network of other luxury property agents and people in the demographics who can afford to purchase the home. Ask to review the marketing materials used to market similar homes and how they propose to expose the home to qualified buyers. Also inquire how they vet potential buyers to make sure that they can realistically afford the property.

The time working with an agent can often be an intense experience and there is often quite a bit at stake, so it's especially important to choose an experienced agent who is going to be watching out for your best interests and has the reputation of always working in an ethical and professional manner. At the end of the day, you are hiring an expert that should be able to take care of their business professionally so you don't have to worry about everything yourself.

## About Elena Price

Elena Price has successfully sold real estate for over 25 years. She is affiliated with Coldwell Banker Residential Brokerage's Westwood, Massachusetts office in the suburban Boston area. Her focus is on assisting sellers and buyers of luxury residences in Westwood, Dover, Needham, Dedham, and Walpole.

Elena has been ranked in the Top 1% of real estate agents in the nation. She has also been recognized and has won a number of awards for sales excellence including Top 10 in New England for Coldwell Banker Residential Brokerage,

International Presidents Premier Club, and Top 20 Club of Coldwell Banker Residential Brokerage of New England.

Elena is a Global Luxury Specialist, Coldwell Banker's top designation for brokers and agents qualified to sell luxury properties. She is also a Certified Relocation Specialist, Certified Buyers Representative, and Certified New Homes Specialist.

Elena frequently is interviewed and featured on news media as a local real estate expert. She has appeared on WBZ NewsRadio, the Home & Garden TV Network's "House Hunters" show, the "In Style Boston" TV show, and the WBNW 1120am Radio show, "Money Matters."

For more information about Elena Price, visit https://www.ElenaPrice.com.

# Buying and Selling Luxury Homes in Ventura County and the San Fernando Valley

# Alex Gandel

## Introduction

Alex Gandel is an award-winning, top producing real estate agent affiliated with Century 21 Troop Real Estate in Simi Valley, California. He helps clients buy and sell homes in Ventura County and in the San Fernando Valley communities of Los Angeles County in Southern California. Alex and his staff work with clients in all price ranges and he has extensive experience representing buyers and sellers of luxury and estate properties in the area.

In this chapter, Alex elaborates on the most important factors for buyers and sellers of luxury properties in Ventura County and the San Fernando Valley.

## Selling Your Luxury Home

There is a tremendous pride in home ownership, and selling one's home is an emotional experience. An important key is to not let emotional attachment overly influence the business aspects of selling a home. When meeting with sellers for the first time, the initial consideration is usually the value of their home. Statistics, such as price per square foot, play a part in analyzing value; however, these numbers can't tell the whole story. An experienced agent will advise on the likely market value of a property based on various factors, including the market situation and the prices of several of the most closely comparable recent sales, adjusted for amenities and other factors.

When it comes to luxury and estate properties, they are all custom or customized to some extent with different amenities, all of which lead to a different value. Amenities that make a difference in value include the location, view, privacy, privately gated versus non-gated community, pool, spa, tennis court, level of interior finishes, landscaping and hardscaping, as well as other factors. The age and style of finishes in the home also influence the value. Given that the home probably was customized according to the preferences of the owner, keep in mind that not everyone's tastes are the same and the value attributed to the features will vary by individual. Some costly upgrades may have little value when it's time to sell. On the other hand, very attractive features like an amazing swimming pool may be more valuable to some buyers — and they may even attribute more value to an amenity than an appraiser would.

A lot of my work in determining value involves analyzing comparable recent sales in the area and making adjustments for size, location, age, features, and condition. One of the challenges when comparing sales is to understand the condition of the prior sales. As an example, if a prior sale was related to a distress situation, such as a divorce, trust sale, or a tax sale, it might have sold for a lower amount than under a different situation. An analysis that includes all of the pertinent factors gives us an opportunity to create a more accurate assessment of the value and hopefully removes part of the emotion that goes into the seller's decision on pricing.

It's critical as we start to market a home that the property is show-ready and is going to draw buyers into the yard and the home itself. Everything needs to look fresh, inviting, and well maintained. You only have one chance to make a first impression and that starts right at the curb. Everything should be looked at through a buyer's eyes. If there's a burned-out light bulb, cobwebs, or stains, buyers are likely to wonder what else is wrong that they can't see. It's a matter of detailing the property, and depending on the situation, it can be done in a series of steps.

Initially, review the yard and exterior from the curb to the back fence. The landscaping needs to be tidy, with the lawn mowed, weeds removed, and fresh mulch applied, if needed. If the driveway has stains, it would be wise to have them removed. The outside accent lighting should be working correctly so when potential buyers drive by in the evening they can see how beautiful the house looks lit up. Outside fountains should also be working. Adding color with flowering plants always helps make a yard more attractive.

Starting at the front entry, take a critical walk around the exterior of the house. Cobwebs should be removed and the windows cleaned. The house should be pressure washed if there are any stains or if it needs to be cleaned. Often the paint needs to be touched up, and sometimes the exterior should be repainted.

Walk through the home room by room to see what can be done to make it look as perfect as possible. Carpets need to be cleaned and paint should be touched up if there are scratches. It's important to take care of small details like vacuuming the return grills for the furnaces and air conditioning. If you have pets, there will be odors. Some people who have cats or dogs don't notice the odors because they live with them every day, but visitors will notice the smell. Pet odors need to be reduced as much as possible.

For most homeowners, one of the top challenges is decluttering. Most people accumulate a large amount of stuff over time, and it doesn't feel like home without the counters, shelves, and walls covered with personal effects.

The problem with a cluttered house is that buyers have a hard time imagining living in a home that's filled with another family's personal items. They end up focusing on the seller's belongings rather than on the house itself. A cluttered home also looks smaller, so buyers may not think their furnishing will fit. Closet space is also a common concern. It's better to clear out your closets so that they appear to have plenty of room. Since you're going to be selling and moving, you'll have to pack at some point. This is really a perfect time to organize a good portion of your personal items and store them until the move. Finally, the garage should also be free of clutter so that it's easy for buyers to visualize their car parked there and imagine how their belongings will fit in the space.

Most of what we have discussed doesn't involve much investment, but there are times when more significant spending is warranted to be able to obtain top dollar from the sale. As an example, an outdated kitchen is a concern to most buyers, so they may subtract more value from the home than an updated kitchen would cost. Before spending money on major renovations, however, I would advise that you have an expert review the situation and estimate the likely cost and expected sale price increase to make sure an investment will create enough additional value. Of course, this also depends on the sellers' objectives and willingness to make such an investment. Sometimes sellers are just not willing to put additional money into the home and will sell it "as is" and let the buyer make those changes on their own after the home is sold.

There are times when a seller has already moved and the home is vacant when it is being put on the market. Most buyers don't have the vision to see how their furnishing will fit in empty rooms, so we recommend staging the home with furnishings. There is a cost involved with staging, but we have found it to be an effective tool. We also have a virtual staging concept in which furniture is virtually placed within photos of the empty rooms so buyers can better visualize how the rooms look when furnished. These photos are used online (with appropriate disclosure), and we also place an easel with the photo in the empty room so buyers can visualize the filled room as they are walking through the home.

Most people are finding and looking at homes online, so accurate and professional photography is critical to maximize the visual impact of a home and display all of the amenities. Just like an in-person showing, there are only a few seconds to make that first impression. Our photographer will typically take 120 to 140 photos so we can pick the best ones to show in our listings. Evening photos often show a home in attractive lighting, so we tend to use some of these as well as aerial photos, which are important when there is a great view or property setting to display. We also organize a 3D virtual tour for our luxury listings so viewers can get a feel for walking through the home.

We create an eight-page custom color magazine for our luxury home listings with a selection of photos as well as a room-by-room description of the home, detailing all of the features. This is a great way for people who have been through the home to remember all of the details.

We never really know where a buyer is going to come from, so it's important to use a wide variety of marketing channels to attract our ideal buyer. Online advertising is critical, and many of the major sites have reciprocal arrangements with the multiple listing services, but there is a challenge in making sure they are all accurate, which takes some dedication and effort. I also advertise on my own website as well as our agency website. We also put our luxury listings on the Century 21 Luxury Home website as well as the Century 21 regular website. Facebook and Google ads have also proven to be effective.

Text marketing is another approach we have recently adopted. If the home has a sign in front, we place a number on the sign so that potential buyers can text for additional information. After sending the text message, the website for the listing appears on the phone. We also now have a number to call for follow-up with someone who has indicated interest. I've also found that some traditional advertising methods are still working. As an example, I do newspaper advertising and announce listings with press releases that often get picked up in the real estate section of local newspapers. Although newspaper circulation has declined, there are still a lot of people who read their local paper and get their news and information through that medium. I also use billboard advertising at local car washes.

We have a number of additional techniques we use, including catered broker open houses, office caravans, email blasts to agents and brokers in Ventura and Los Angeles Counties, email blasts to people who have indicated interest in purchasing a home, and advertising in luxury real estate magazines. There is some debate about the effectiveness of open houses; however, recently one of the people on our email list showed up to an open house as a result of an announcement in an email. The gentleman spent two hours at the open house and by the end of the next day wrote a check for $1.7 million to purchase the house.

The busiest time of the year for home sales in our area is typically January through June, although there is activity throughout the year. At the higher end, we see activity related to job transfers that can happen at any time of the year, so there's really no bad time to list a luxury property here in Southern California. There is usually a lull in activity from Thanksgiving to the end of the year throughout the holidays, but people looking at that time are generally serious buyers.

One of my policies is for me, or a seasoned staff member, to be present at our showings so we can ensure that potential buyers are not missing any of the finer details about the property. The buyer's agent may not be as familiar with the particular community and thus may not be able to provide enough local information to help the buyer make a decision. Details about the benefits of living in that particular location, including information about the local schools, distance to shopping and restaurants, and commute times, are all important to buyers. This knowledge is not so obvious, and it can be very beneficial in bringing a buyer around to considering the property.

The culmination of our preparation and marketing efforts is one or more offers from prospective buyers, but that is just the start of the negotiating process. My job as seller's agent is to keep the negotiations flowing so we can get the sale closed. It's important for the seller to keep an open mind so that we can ultimately have a win-win transaction that both the buyer and seller are happy with. It can take one counter-offer or it may take six, but it's important that all parties stay calm and try to remove emotions as much as possible from the negotiations. Before we even make a counter-offer, we want to understand the financial ability of the buyer to close on the transaction so that we know we are dealing with a real buyer. If there is financing involved, we want to review pre-approval documents from their lender. Sometimes we request that the buyer speak with our lender as well to increase our comfort level. Frequently, luxury home purchases are all-cash transactions, so we want to see proof of funds in the form of a bank statement or other documentation before we respond to an offer.

Once the final agreement is negotiated, it's generally going to be a minimum of 30 to 45 days to close the escrow if there is financing required. With an all-cash purchase, it can be as short as one or two weeks, depending on the terms of the agreement between the buyer and the seller and whether or not there is a Home Owners Association (HOA). There will be a period for the buyer to remove contingencies such as for inspections, approval of HOA by-laws and financials, and CC&R's.

## What Sellers Are Saying

*"What can I say other than selling our home with Alex and his incredible team could not have gone any smoother. At our initial meeting, Alex brought a comprehensive presentation of his experience and services as well as our local comparable market. He immediately honed in on how to best address selling our home and was very attentive to our needs every step of the way. His experience, marketing strategies, personal nature and wonderful team made Alex the best possible choice to sell our home!"*
    - Shelly M.

*"Mr. Alex Gandel is a very knowledgeable, polite and professional agent. There are many real estate agents in the area but what makes him better than the rest in the area is the fact that he gives a lot of effort in each and every listing he has to sell. When we met him for the first time, we were extremely impressed by the amount of research he had already put in to know the value of our house and the additional information needed to sell. He was very informative as well. He comes across as a very calm person who exactly knows what he is doing and confident about it as well. He is a marketing machine and once our house was in the market, he left no stone*

*unturned to advertise our listing! We thank Alex and his team from the bottom of our heart and will use his services in future as well and recommend him to our friends in the area. We wish Alex and his team the very best in their future endeavors."*
    - Soumya and Binay D.

*"Alex is a great realtor and great person. He has so much knowledge, he is thoughtful, he cares about his clients, he is generous with his time, and he just has a kind peaceful way about him. Not only did Alex do an amazing job selling our house in 2 days but he has a team that is superb! They are extremely professional, efficient, and they all reflect the calm and caring attributes that Alex demonstrates. We are past clients of Alex and we would not use any other broker. He really is the best."*
    - Bobbi and Lance K.

## Buying Your Luxury Home

The first step in looking for a home is to think through all of your needs and put them in priority order — things like general location, type of community, school system, traffic and commute time, amenities, and so on. Of course, an important consideration is the amount of money you're comfortable spending as that's going to be a key factor in the specific locations you will consider.

Most buyers decide to work with a buyer's agent to help them find a home and to represent them through the transaction because they believe a buyer's agent will work on their behalf better than working directly with a listing agent. In fact, the listing agent has a fiduciary responsibility to the seller, so a buyer will not obtain any special benefit by not using a buyer's agent. However, contacting the listing agent could work to your benefit in a seller's market when inventory levels are low. If the buyer is moving from another area of the country, an experienced agent will be able to provide details about the local area that are not necessarily available from other sources, including online.

It's important to share your objectives and priorities with your agent so that the agent can help you find the best fit. After a discussion about the priorities, I like to take buyers on a tour of a few available properties during the first meeting to get some feedback and to better understand what they are trying to accomplish. Many times the tour uncovers additional needs that weren't initially expressed. People coming from a different part of the country may be accustomed to more traditional housing styles instead of the open floor plans typically seen in this area. They also may have lived on larger pieces of property that are not common in Southern California metro areas. The brief tour may change some of the perceptions of the buyers and help them recalibrate their objectives.

If mortgage financing is going to be used to acquire a home, it needs to be lined up in advance with a pre-approval. First, sellers are not likely to consider an offer that is subject to obtaining financing, if not already approved, and second, the level of financing ability is likely to be a large factor in the price of a home that can be afforded. Property values along with certain lifestyles and amenities vary widely among different locations in this area, so understanding what can be afforded in advance will save a lot of time in finding a home that will best fit your needs. Sometimes after seeing various communities and getting a feel for the pricing, the objectives may need to be adjusted based on property values in certain communities.

Once buyers have narrowed down available properties to one or a few, we will help them assess the fair market value. I will go through a comparative market analysis similar to what I do for a seller to advise on the estimated value of one or more of the properties the buyer is interested in pursuing. There are websites that provide an estimate of value, but those are not typically very accurate. First, it's important to make sure the statistical information in the descriptions online as well as past sales prices shown are accurate. Without verification of the data, through the title company or verification of the tax-transfer stamps, it's not possible to know if the sales data shown is correct. As mentioned earlier, we also need to know the condition of the sales of comparable properties we are using in our analysis. I can generally get this information from the listing agents of the prior sales. Appraisers are pretty rigid in the manner in which they perform their appraisals for lenders. If the buyer is going to be using financing, I will also consider how an appraiser is likely to value a property. As an example, a property that has a beautiful pool that would cost $150,000 to $200,000 to install or replace may have that much value to the owner and certain buyers. Unfortunately, an appraiser may limit the value placed on the pool at only $50,000 due to a belief that the pool reflects an over-improvement for the property or it has depreciated in value due to its age. This information can be important in determining a price to offer, as the buyer typically doesn't want to offer more than what the lender's appraisal is likely to come in at.

Sellers are generally going to only consider or counter offers that they deem as strong and from well-qualified buyers, so we will include a pre-approval letter to present with the offer. I also recommend that buyers write a letter about themselves to present to the sellers with the offer to explain who they are and why they are interested in buying the home. We write a letter about the buyers ourselves, discussing how we met them and our experience with them through the home search process. We also indicate that we are offering our assistance in trying to bring the two parties together in the best possible manner and that we will be available by phone at all times. We typically include financials, bank statements, and maybe credit scores, and we delete account numbers and Social Security numbers. Generally speaking, we don't have an opportunity to sit in front of a seller and explain why they should select our buyers to purchase their home, so this is a way to build credibility that our buyers are serious. This information is important to a seller who is going to take the property off the market during the contingency period.

Flexibility in negotiations always depends on the seller, but the market conditions generally influence the pace of negotiations as well. If the demand is lower and we are in a buyer's market, sellers tend to be more flexible as there aren't many buyers. As the market becomes more balanced, sellers become less flexible, and during periods of high demand without adequate supply — in a seller's market — sellers may get to choose among multiple offers, so there's not going to be much flexibility. In a tight seller's market, sellers may be unwilling to accept contingencies beyond inspections. As this is being written, we have been in a seller's market, and I recommend that buyers take their best shot in making an offer if they truly want the house, especially if the home is competitively priced and is likely to attract multiple offers. You don't want to look back and think that ten thousand dollars, or whatever the number might be, kept you from purchasing the house you really wanted. It may still not be enough, but at least you know that you made the best offer you could, it just was not meant to be, and there will be a better property for you.

A common complication arises when a buyer needs to sell an existing house in order to free up money for a down payment on a new home. The most straightforward sequence is to sell the current home, get the cash out, move to a temporary home, find and purchase the new home, and then move again. Since two moves are required, this is not a popular sequence. An ideal sequence would be to make an offer to purchase a home and make it contingent on selling the existing home. This is easy for the person wanting to sell their existing home and move to a new home, but sellers are not likely to make their sale contingent upon the buyer having to sell their home to an unknown buyer.

One solution is for the party wanting to sell and move to put their home on the market. Once a buyer is identified, they can start looking for a new home. It's important that the first buyer is well qualified with verifiable information and that the sale is not subject to contingencies. It's preferable in this case to set a longer escrow period, at least 60 days, to allow enough time to find a new property. Another possibility is to make the first sale contingent on the seller finding and purchasing a new home. In either case, the escrow on the two sales would close together. It's critical to work with an agent experienced in complex transactions when considering this approach.

## What Buyers Are Saying

*"My husband and I were moving from Woodland Hills to Ventura County. We worked with Alex Gandel and his son, Brad, to purchase our first home as we heard great things about his knowledge of the Simi Valley, Moorpark, and Camarillo areas. Alex took time to explain each step in the home buying process to us and made sure we didn't jump into a property too quickly. The house that we ended up purchasing was made known to us as Alex had a personal connection with the seller and got us into the house on day 1. My*

husband and I were really impressed with Alex's responsiveness and we enjoyed getting to work with his son and team as well. I would definitely recommend Alex Gandel as a realtor!"
   - Nicole S.

"Alex Gandel is the most knowledgeable and professional agent I have known. Alex represented us in buying our current house in 2009, and we consider him our friend. Currently, he's helping us with our next purchase. With Alex we found what we were looking for in an agent: peace of mind, and knowledge that the transaction will be handled extremely proficiently without us getting involved in, and worrying about the details. We greatly appreciate Alex's and his team's handling of this sale and will definitely use their services in future, and recommend them to our friends."
   - Vic N.

"Once again, Alex and Staff did a great job for us. The purchase process went smoothly after Alex found us a great house. We love it, but if we ever decide to sell it, Alex will be the Realtor we call."
   - Robert and Virginia B.

## Selecting the Best Agent for You

Whether buying or selling a luxury property, it's an emotional, challenging, and intense process. There will be significant communications required during the transaction, and I would suggest finding an agent that you sense has a compatible personality and is someone you can trust. You may need to interview more than one agent before finding the one that seems to be a good fit for you. Sales of luxury properties are complex transactions with a lot of money at stake, so experience in luxury property sales in the area is a key factor to check. Experienced professionals have a list of references that should be checked, and reviews and testimonials are another indicator of success. Referrals from other luxury homeowners, bankers, or business professionals can be a good source of recommended agents.

An important question to ask an agent candidate if you are selling is "How do you plan to market my property?" Is the agent willing and able to invest in multiple marketing channels, both online as well as offline? As I discussed earlier, we really don't know where a buyer is going to come from, and if your property is not going to be presented in a variety of media, the ideal buyer may not find the property. An agent should portray passion as well confidence in representing the property to other agents and buyers. As we move into the higher price range homes, the pool of qualified buyers diminishes. It's not going to provide any benefit to a seller if the agent is not actively using all means possible to constantly fish for the right buyer.

Real estate is a very local business, and local knowledge is a critical element, especially when a buyer from out of the area is interested in purchasing a home. Knowledge of schools and scores, traffic and commute times, proximity to shopping and restaurants, lifestyle options, and other local details are all important for buyers, and there is no substitute for an experienced agent who can guide you through the information.

## About Alex Gandel

After studying real estate marketing, finance and economics in college, Alex Gandel embarked on a career in real estate sales. He has been a top producer since he started in real estate in 1980 and has consistently earned esteemed awards from his company and the community for his outstanding performance and passionate leadership. In 2017, Alex earned a place among the top 10 Century 21 Agents nationwide. In January of 2018 Alex was awarded with the "Business Person of the Year" award for 2017 from the Simi Valley Chamber of Commerce.

Alex is affiliated with Century 21 Troop Real Estate in Simi Valley, California. He and his staff help buyers and sellers in all price ranges in eastern Ventura County and in the adjacent San Fernando Valley of Los Angeles County. In addition to working with standard real estate transactions he frequently assists clients in challenging circumstances, such as divorce situations, short sales, and other hardship transactions. Alex also helps clients with complex transactions including contingent sales with a home of choice, exchanges for investors, and relocations.

Alex willingly shares his experience and knowledge with others in the industry as a frequent speaker at real estate and mortgage panels and conferences.

For more information about Alex Gandel, visit www.AlexGandel.com.

www.ingramcontent.com/pod-product-compliance
Lightning Source LLC
Chambersburg PA
CBHW071534220526
45469CB00003B/773